Advance Praise for *The Road to Healing*

"Reparation" is a buzzword, even in the case of educations lost for victims of Virginia's monstrous campaign of massive resistance of sixty years ago, the goal of which was to defeat the integration of public schools. But as Ken Woodley tells in *The Road to Healing*, a plan to provide scholarships to compensate for a five-year shutdown of these schools helped spur racial reconciliation in the state's Prince Edward County, thus proving the value of such efforts. This remarkable book describes both an important episode in our civil rights history and how enlightened leadership helped heal the wounds it caused.

> — CURTIS WILKIE, Overby Fellow and Kelly G. Cook Chair of
> Journalism at the University of Mississippi, author of *Dixie: A
> Personal Odyssey Through Events That Shaped the Modern South*

Ken Woodley provides a powerful insider's account of the struggle to establish Virginia's *Brown v. Board of Education* Scholarship Program to provide academic opportunities for those denied an education by their own elected officials during the massive resistance years. Probing the nature of reconciliation and the still-open wounds of racially motivated school closings, Woodley powerfully reminds readers that real apologies demand tangible action, and that while the past cannot be changed, the present most certainly can.

> — JILL OGLINE TITUS, author of *Brown's Battleground:
> Students, Segregationists, and the Struggle for
> Justice in Prince Edward County, Virginia*

Talk about speaking truth to power! As the editor of a small-town, family-owned newspaper, Ken Woodley crusaded for decades to get his community to renounce its past devotion to segregation, a cause that had been championed before he got there by his own paper. Driven by deep spirituality and tenacious resolve, Woodley not only succeeded, but persuaded the Virginia legislature to pay reparations to the victims.

> — DONALD P. BAKER, retired *Washington Post* journalist
> and author of *Wilder: Hold Fast to Dreams*, the
> biography of America's first elected black governor

Barbara Johns lit the lamp and Ken Woodley used it to help light the way for the rest of us. That is a lesson worth repeating across every generation. The ultimate lesson of *The Road to Healing* is that you often do not cure the great ills of the world by grand gestures. You start small, and it is always best to begin in your own backyard.

— MARK WARNER, U.S. Senator and former Virginia Governor

As someone who was directly and indirectly affected by the shameful history in Prince Edward County, I truly believe God sent Ken Woodley as one of his shepherds to heal the racial divide and help us move towards reconciliation. *The Road to Healing* is a gripping account—candid and informed—of Woodley's efforts to right a terrible wrong in the wake of what happened in Virginia in the years between 1959 and 1964. An emotional, powerful must-read!

— JOAN JOHNS COBBS, sister of civil rights
history-maker Barbara Rose Johns

Some true stories surpass fiction in their ability to amaze, to inspire, and to impose symmetry on a chaotic world. Ken Woodley's work to bring racial healing to Prince Edward County, Virginia, is one such story. That this small-town newspaper editor did so much good occupying a seat where so much destruction was once sown is a kind of miracle.

— MARGARET EDDS, author of *We Face the Dawn:
Oliver Hill, Spottswood Robinson, and the
Legal Team that Dismantled Jim Crow*

Woodley has been an untiring witness, or in the words of Isaiah, "an ensign of the people," heralding the deeper meaning of the Prince Edward story. *The Road to Healing* shows the extent of that labor, the twists and turns, the compromises and momentary disappointments, and the slowly growing wisdom of a community—indeed an entire nation—turning from past to future. But the work is never done. And we so need examples to help us persevere in that work. I thank Ken Woodley for giving us such an example.

— TIM KAINE, U.S. Senator and former Vice Presidential nominee

THE ROAD TO HEALING

THE ROAD TO HEALING

A Civil Rights Reparations Story in Prince Edward County, Virginia

KEN WOODLEY

FOREWORD BY MARK WARNER

AFTERWORD BY TIM KAINE

NEWSOUTH BOOKS

Montgomery

NewSouth Books
105 S. Court Street
Montgomery, AL 36104

Publisher's Cataloging-in-Publication Data

Woodley, Ken.
The road to healing: a civil rights reparations story in Prince Edward County,
Virginia / Ken Woodley ; foreword by Mark Warner ; afterword by Tim Kaine
p. cm.
Includes photos, bibliography, index.

ISBN 978-1-58838-354-9 (hardcover)
ISBN 978-1-58838-355-6 (ebook)

1. Woodley, Ken. 2. African Americans—Civil rights—Virginia—History—20th
century. 3. African Americans—Civil rights—Southern States—History—20th
century. 4. Civil rights movements—Civil rights—Virginia—History—20th century.
5. Civil rights movements—Civil rights—Southern States—History—20th century.
II. Title.

2018051191

Full Library of Congress Cataloging-in-Publication data available at
www.newsouthbooks.com/roadtohealing.

Design by Randall Williams

Printed in the United States of America by Sheridan Books

*To my wife, Kim,
for saving my life so I could write this book.*

*To John Hurt—locked out of public schools for five years after
the first grade by his own community—for giving it a hero.*

*To U.S. Senator Mark Warner who, as governor
of the Commonwealth of Virginia, stood tallest and strongest
with us when we needed it most.*

*And to Barbara Rose Johns,
for having the courage to dream.*

Contents

Foreword

U.S. SENATOR MARK R. WARNER

One of my heroes, Barbara Johns, is central to the story you are about to read. I never had the privilege of meeting her, but this young woman demonstrated righteous courage and fearless leadership in 1951 when, at the age of sixteen, she organized and led a student walkout to protest conditions at the all-black Robert R. Moton High School in Prince Edward County, Virginia.

Moton was very separate and vastly unequal from the other public schools in the county. Moton held more than twice the number of students it was built to accommodate, yet the local school board refused to build a new high school for African American students. Instead, they erected tarpaper shacks. The rooms were freezing in winter, and water dripped from the ceiling and walls when it rained.

Barbara Johns was justifiably frustrated by the struggles she faced simply to access the free public education guaranteed in the Virginia Constitution to every child born in the Commonwealth. With the help of lawyers from the NAACP, Barbara and the Moton parents filed a civil rights lawsuit to integrate Prince Edward County's public schools.

Their lawsuit ultimately became one of the five cases that the U.S. Supreme Court reviewed in the historic 1954 *Brown v. Board of Education* case, which anchored the Court's historic decision to declare segregation in public education to be fundamentally unconstitutional.

In later years, Barbara Johns was modest about her courage. Our heroes tend to be like that, don't they? "There wasn't any fear," she later said. "I just thought—this is your moment. Seize it."

That same drive is what motivated *Farmville Herald* editor Ken Woodley to push us to establish scholarships for a generation of African American students denied a public education when some public schools in Virginia, and in Prince Edward County the entire public school system, were closed in defiance of the Court's integration decision.

The ultimate lesson of Woodley's *The Road to Healing* is that you often do not cure the great ills of the world by grand gestures: you start small, and it is always best to begin in your own backyard.

I think you will enjoy Woodley's absorbing and detailed account of our combined efforts leading to the 2004 creation of the *Brown* Scholarship program in Virginia. Along the way, *The Road to Healing* also succeeds in documenting nearly three decades of recent Virginia political history as Woodley details his interactions with many of the leading personalities, and discusses the often complicated politics, that got caught up in the effort.

In 2004, our administration was working mightily to win Virginia General Assembly approval for a once-in-a-generation fix for Virginia's structurally unbalanced budget. That larger budget struggle ultimately was successful, after no fewer than three high-stakes special legislative sessions. And by reforming our budget and tax system, Virginia was well positioned to keep its commitments in public education, job creation, public safety, and the protection of our natural resources.

In the following pages, Woodley will put forth his suspicions that during that 2004 budget struggle my personal commitment to the *Brown* Scholarship proposal somehow became diminished. As you will discover, nothing could have been further from the truth.

Once we had secured bipartisan legislative support for our 2004 budget reforms, other budget priorities quickly fell into place—including the *Brown* Scholarship program. That was due, in many ways, to the dogged persistence of Ken Woodley and many others. As you'll also read in Woodley's lively account, the effort also received an unexpected assist from Virginia philanthropist John Kluge, who was moved by news coverage of the goals of the *Brown* Scholarship proposal, and agreed to personally match the state's financial commitment to launch the program.

During my four-year term as Virginia's sixty-ninth governor, I also was pleased to find another opportunity to publicly honor and celebrate the example set by Barbara Johns and her Moton classmates. During an evening stroll early in my tenure in Richmond, my youngest daughter Eliza pointed out that there were a lot of statues on the grounds of the Virginia State Capitol complex: George Washington, Patrick Henry, Stonewall Jackson, and dozens of other Virginia historical figures are there, proudly memorialized in bronze and stone.

My daughter asked a simple, but poignant, question: where were the statues of women? And what about people of color? Her questions prompted us to raise private funds to construct the Virginia Civil Rights Memorial, which stands on Capitol Square in Richmond today. It honors a series of Virginia's heroes—and heroines—in the fight for freedom. Appropriately, the figure of Barbara Johns is a centerpiece of that Memorial.

Dr. Martin Luther King Jr. once said, "If I cannot do great things, I can do small things in a great way." That's certainly what Barbara Johns did: standing up for what was right, no matter the consequences, and changing history as a result. Barbara Johns lit the lamp and, as you'll read in the pages that follow, Ken Woodley used the light from that lamp to help point the way for the rest of us. That is a lesson worth repeating across every generation.

The author with his mother, Lorraine Suggs Woodley, in the yard of the family's home in Farmville in the late 1950s. (Photo by James K. Woodley Jr.)

Preface

I look at a photograph taken in Prince Edward County in the fully bloomed spring of 1959, five years after the U.S. Supreme Court's *Brown v. Board of Education* decision. The world, itself, was unprepared for what was about to happen. Even in this small black-and-white photo it's clear the sky was too blue. The leaves on the trees too green. The sun too warm on the skin. There was no sign of onrushing doom anywhere.

Something inside me still trembles. I see my two-year-old self and the street beyond the front yard of the apartment my parents rented, a few rooms downstairs in one of the neighborhood's Victorian houses. I was born in Farmville, the county seat of Prince Edward County, in 1957 while my father completed his final two years at Hampden-Sydney College, six miles down the road.

Within that photograph, the world appears to be perfect. And it was, for me, with my blond hair, blue eyes and white skin. They were my passport to any seat on the bus, any lunch-counter stool—liberty and justice for me. I hold that apparent Eden in the palm of my hand with great care, as if it were a priceless artifact. In fact, it is the rarest and most impossible of artifacts.

In the picture, the world looks just the way God made it. But the snapshot lies. It is an artifact of a world that did not exist, even as the shutter captured it on film.

Such black-and-white photographs were the only way those colors were ever integrated in Farmville in the 1950s. Beyond the border of those photos Prince Edward County was about to shatter for African American children. The sun would still shine indiscriminately from a blue sky and through green leaves onto the community's children. But the sun would be alone in doing so.

There I am, a happy child playing on a tree-shaded lawn on High Street. But just four blocks away, turning left on Main Street, the county's Board of Supervisors was poised to shut down an entire public school system and keep it closed for five years. Minds would stay closed even longer.

I had never heard of massive resistance when I arrived to work at the *Farmville Herald* following my May 1979 graduation from Hampden-Sydney College. I had no idea Prince Edward County's public school system had been shut down. Nor did I know that the newspaper at which I had just been hired led the public fight to lock those school doors.

My ignorance was the product of design. The American history contributed by African Americans was confined to brief glimpses as I'd grown up. Their agony and achievements were generally no more than footnotes in the voluminous history told by whites.

I was born there and lived Farmville for the first two years of my life. But my parents were natives of Richmond. We lived in Farmville only until my father graduated from college in May 1959. Prince Edward County is located in the central-southern Piedmont of Virginia. Tobacco was king. So was segregation. My father proudly received his diploma and two weeks later—just as Prince Edward County's Board of Supervisors was preparing to eradicate the public school system—moved to Richmond, where I was raised.

When I learned what had happened in Prince Edward County, and the *Farmville Herald's* role in massive resistance, I felt that life had parachuted me behind enemy lines. How could I stay and work for this newspaper? The same family owned it. The same pro-massive resistance editorial writer—the newspaper's publisher—was in place. Had I known any of that, I never would have applied for the job. I never would have walked through the door for any reason whatsoever.

I attended two schools with student bodies that were 80 to 90 percent black from fall 1970 to summer 1973 during court-ordered busing to achieve integration in the city of Richmond's public schools. Those three years confirmed the belief I'd had since I was a small child that people are people. The color of someone's skin had no deep meaning for me. It was just skin.

I had a crush on one of my English teachers at Thomas Jefferson High School, the young and beautiful Miss Lewis. Most of the boys did. On the last day of the 1972 school year I brought my camera and took her picture. Miss Lewis was black.

I might have run like hell at the first opportunity to leave the *Farmville Herald*. I nearly did. But through the cacophony of those emotions I felt a quiet call to stay, to somehow find a way to use this newspaper to help heal the wound it had done so much to create. But what could I do? What could anyone do? Was I on some delusional, ego-driven wild goose chase?

A 1994 letter from Oliver Hill, the legendary civil rights attorney, was a foundational moment in my life. The great attorney, whose statue stands in Richmond, and who, along with Barbara Rose Johns, is one of those honored by the Virginia Civil Rights Memorial at the state capitol, wrote this to me:

> I thank you for sending me copies of your well written news statement and brilliant editorial pertaining to the recent celebration of the fortieth anniversary of the *Brown* decision.
>
> It was one of the tragedies of the times that during the fifties and succeeding years we did not have more people with your insight and sensitivity to help work out solutions to our racial problems in . . . Prince Edward County, in Virginia and in the rest of the United States.
>
> I will be quoting from your writings from time to time as I speak on these racial problems."

Those words from that man blew breath on the flame already burning deep inside me. To this day, I feel that letter was my ordination as a minister of racial healing and reconciliation, a laying-on of hands, a commissioning. Hill knighted me as surely as my early childhood imaginings saw King Arthur doing, tapping me on both shoulders with Excalibur in his quest to find the Holy Grail. But, rather than give me a sword, Hill empowered my pen to fullest effect.

The letter revealed that the calling I felt to use the editorial pages of the

Farmville Herald to help bridge the wounding chasm massive resistance had left in the county was not an ego-driven fantasy of self-delusion.

Oliver Hill—*he* was going to be quoting *me*?!—made it clear that any ability I had to express my heart was a gift from God and I had been placed in the middle of the community that needed it most. The newspaper had used its position of influence on behalf of separating the races through massive resistance. I sought to amplify the volume of its editorial pages to unite a deeply wounded community in a journey of recovery *toward* one another. That dream surely was not mine alone, but only one dreamer in the community was lucky enough to be the editor and editorial writer of this newspaper.

The *Brown* decision, I wrote in that May 20, 1994, editorial,

> is something to celebrate and cherish or else America's founding ideals as expressed in the Declaration of Independence and the Constitution are no more than gnats in a strong wind. Those eighteenth-century words, which meant nothing in the lives of African Americans, were given a touch of legitimacy by the Supreme Court's decision on May 17, 1954.

The nation's founding documents and *Brown* mean something, I continued, because they are

> more than a collection of words on paper. The words were keys that began unlocking a series of doors closed and rusted on their hinges.
>
> For African Americans, "No taxation without representation" meant much more in 1954 than it had meant to the colonists two hundred years earlier. The reality of America in the mid-twentieth century, juxtaposed against the idealism of its founding in 1776, revealed a heavy irony in the iron chains society forged, visibly invisible, to lock African Americans out of their birth right as American citizens. All men created equal and endowed by their creator with certain unalienable rights? Among those life, liberty and the pursuit of happiness?
>
> *Brown v. Board* was instrumental in taking the unwritten lie out of those words.

In its own way, the exchange of words from the heart between Hill and me was a microcosm of what I was determined to strive for within Prince Edward County. It was a pivotal moment for me because it demonstrated that my hopes, and the dream of Barbara Rose Johns, were within reach. Hill would be quoting the editor of the *Farmville Herald* as he spoke about our nation's continuing racial problems. This time, Hill would not be condemning what an editor of the *Farmville Herald* had written, but praising it, embracing it.

Oliver Hill would be quoting a newspaper that once had been the bitterest of enemies to the cause he had fought for in court on behalf of the black community of Prince Edward County. This showed me that the world could indeed turn toward a new day. There can be racial reconciliation. There can be healing. We can live, as Barbara Rose Johns dreamed, happily ever after. Or, at least we can join together in the pursuit of happiness.

As I looked back on my life while writing this book, trying to decode the origin of my racial sensibilities, I knew that my first experience with African Americans was classically stereotypical. My maternal grandfather was a well-to-do physician in Richmond and had a live-in cook/housekeeper six days a week, as well as a gardener. From infancy onward, I had a great deal of contact with them both, especially with Helen Byrd. I would spend hours playing with a wooden train set in the laundry room just off the kitchen, where she spent much of her day.

But there was a twist in the stereotype: That man and that woman performed jobs that my own parents did. Robert Hatchett cut the grass, just as my father did at our home. Helen cooked and did the laundry, just like my mom. There was nothing menial or subservient about it to my eyes. Black or white, you cut the grass and cleaned the house.

As I was filing away thirty-six years of papers from my career at the newspaper, I found a copy of a letter I had written to Helen Byrd in January of 2004 when my attempt to bring healing to the wound of massive resistance was entering the General Assembly. She was living in the Tidewater area and I hadn't seen her since my grandmother's funeral thirty years earlier, when I was still in high school. I had wanted her to know what I was doing, and why:

You have always been an important part of my life. You were the first African American I met in this world and in my life and I was just a few years old. As a I child I could immediately sense the love and warmth inside you and the human dignity. And that only grew as I grew older. Yes, I love the memory of those little biscuits you cooked and served when I spent the night with Dr. and Mrs. Suggs, my grandparents, but I love the memory of my time with you as a person much, much more.

After spending time with you, for the rest of my life I could never believe the lies of those who disrespect people because of the color of their skin. I've never known a better person than you, Helen."

Color never mattered to me, and I thank God for that truth in my life.

Despite being a licensed lay preacher in the Episcopal Church, I do not consider myself a religious person. Spiritual, but not dogmatic.

God is love. This is the three-word core of Jesus's ministry, a diamond the world, including some aspects of organized religion, surrounds with coal. We are meant to love one another. By doing so we can bring God's love into our own lives and into the lives of those with whom we share this world. We can spend our lives nurturing the God-given "christ" flame within us, ignoring it or trying to snuff it out. Life is that easy and that difficult.

I aspire to that spiritual path. God literally knows I often wander off and get lost, but my spirituality and faith were my core inner resources during the sixteen months of the *Brown* Scholarship Crusade. I do not aim to preach religion at anyone in this book but that part of me must be stated or this book will not tell the truth.

A few days after telling him about my legislative plan for reparations during our phone conversation on February 18, 2003, I received a follow-up note from my friend John Stokes, a man with whom I began developing a lifelong friendship in the late 1990s as the Robert Russa Moton Museum project caught his attention and began healing some of the places in his heart and soul that hurt so deeply.

"Brother," he had typed in all-caps letters, "you are indeed a blessing from God. I have prayed that God would send me someone who would know how to handle this situation.

"Thank God for you."

I thanked God, after reading Stokes's words, that the two-year-old boy playing in that spring of 1959 Polaroid photograph had found his way back to Prince Edward.

But there is something else about that photograph. Looking at it, I realized that J. Barrye Wall Sr. had lived three blocks away. The *Farmville Herald's* publisher would have driven past our apartment every morning on his way to write pro-massive resistance editorials in 1957, 1958, and 1959—before my parents moved to Richmond—and then again on his way home after publishing them.

Managing editor John C. Steck—a member of the school-closing Prince Edward County Board of Supervisors—lived one block away. He also would have passed our High Street residence during his short drive to and from the *Farmville Herald*.

The child they may have occasionally noticed playing on the lawn would spend his career at J. Barrye Wall Sr.'s newspaper trying to repair the harm.

My return to the county had been improbable. I applied for admission to four Virginia colleges. Only my father's alma mater, Hampden-Sydney—the small all-male liberal arts college had not been my first, second or third choice—accepted me. I had to come back. Hampden-Sydney College proved to be a perfect fit, however, in so many ways. Writing for its student newspaper pointed me toward a career in journalism but the lone job offer after graduation was from the *Farmville Herald*. I couldn't leave. Looking at that photo—and thinking about my life's journey—it sometimes felt like destiny. Sometimes it still does.

There is an effective antidote to chest-pounding self-righteousness, however: the thought that had I been born fifty-seven years earlier to different parents, I might have applauded Wall's pro-massive resistance editorials. Or I could have written them.

Barbara Rose Johns's younger sister, Joan, would write these words to me in a 2014 email, a copy of which I keep in my Bible: "I truly believe that God placed you there for a reason." When I answered that I, too, felt that "God had led me all my life to be here," Joan replied: "You know, Ken, reading your comments brought me to tears, as I see that you, too, believe that God meant for you to be there . . . I really wish you could have known my sister, Barbara—a woman of great courage and faith in God—as I believe that you are, as a man. I believe that you two would have had some very interesting, insightful and spiritual conversations."

Of that I am certain. One of the things Barbara Rose Johns and I would talk about is this: I believe, and I'm certain she'd agree, that God wants all of us to act as if we were meant to be exactly where we are, to live as if destiny had called us to be on that very spot, wherever we find ourselves, and to live with healing, loving purpose. I was in Prince Edward County, Virginia and that is all I had tried to do.

"You brought a light to Prince Edward County that nobody thought they'd see," John Stokes told me when my thirty-six-year career at the *Farmville Herald* came to end. Spending my entire journalism career in that community brought a light into my own life that I never thought *I* would see. This is my story of how that light came to shine on, and through, us all.

Acknowledgments

This book is based on my daily *Brown* Scholarship crusade journal, emails, notes, and press clippings. But nobody knows better than I that no man or woman is an island. There are many "I's" in this story. This is my first-person account. But there was and is an entire alphabet around that "I." I was blessed to have some ideas, but the greater blessing—for the whole community, and me—was all of the people who gathered their light with mine to make the ideas real.

My wife, Kim, rock and base camp for all of my "mountaintop journeys." She made my imagined life real, and it exceeded anything I could imagine.

My daughter, Kate, and son, Ian. Being their father continues to deepen me in ways I cannot express.

Ralph Eubanks became a guide, mentor, and finally my agent, leading these words to their own "promised land" at NewSouth Books, co-founded by editor-in-chief Randall Williams and publisher Suzanne La Rosa. I could not have imagined a more welcoming embrace than I received from them. Williams was everything I could have possibly hoped for in an editor, and more: perceptive, sensitive, and wise. I also thank production manager Matthew Byrne for his line-by-line diligence and professionalism, Kelsie Kato for indexing assistance, and Lisa Harrison, NewSouth's publicist, for amplifying this book's voice.

So many helped me on this journey: John Hurt, John Stokes, Joan Johns Cobbs, Rita Odom-Moseley, Helen Byrd, Robert Hatchett, Linwood Davis, Mark R. Warner, Ellen Qualls, A. Linwood Holton, Charles S. Robb, Gerald

L. Baliles, L. Douglas Wilder, George F. Allen, James S. Gilmore, William J. Howell, John Kluge, Viola Baskerville, Benjamin Lambert, Henry Marsh, Brenda Edwards, Clarke Hogan, Shelia Bradley, the Reverend J. Samuel Williams, Dr. Ed Peeples, the Reverend Michael B. Ferguson, William G. Fore, Mattie P. Wiley, Wade Bartlett, Dorothy Holcomb, Leslie Francis "Skip" Griffin Jr., Watkins M. Abbitt Jr., Jerry Kilgore, Tim Murtaugh, Mike Thomas, Frank Atkinson, Russ Potts, Donald P. Baker, Jo Becker, Pamela Stallsmith, Jeff Schapiro, Kevin Hall, Tessa Simonds, Ilah Hickman and Kathryn Braley, Sarah Terry, Oliver Hill, Lorraine and Jim Woodley, and Sarah Elam Puckett.

My dedicated, talented, and good-hearted news staff teammates through the years at the *Farmville Herald,* as well as the production crew responsible for putting our words into print and delivering them to our readers. And William B. Wall and Steven E. Wall, who gave me the editorial pulpit and leadership of the news team.

I gratefully acknowledge Farmville Newsmedia LLC, doing business as The Farmville Herald, for permission to quote excerpts from material published in and by the *Farmville Herald* from 1954 to 2015.

I was fortunate to have these people read versions of the manuscript, offering encouragement, wise criticism and acting as a sounding board: Dr. Ronald Heinemann, Margaret Peters, Karen Owen (copy editing), Karen Simonds, and R. C. Smith.

Jesus shepherded me to God's love and grace since I was a child and God has been present to me through all of the people I have named here, and everyone I have forgotten to name. I feel God's presence in the entirety of this book's story. I am no island. All of you are my continent and helped me gather my light.

THE ROAD TO HEALING

"Harvest is past, summer is over,
And we are not saved.
I am wounded at the sight of my people's wound:
I go like a mourner, overcome by horror.
Is there no balm in Gilead,
no physician there?
Why has no new skin grown over their wound?"
— Jeremiah 8:20–22. The New English Bible
(Cambridge University Press)

Prologue

They closed their schools. Every single one. For five years. On a June day in 1959, Prince Edward County, Virginia, deliberately destroyed public education. I was born there, went to college there, and spent my entire professional career there. And I still can't believe it happened.

The locked classrooms were the nightmare reaction to the dreams African Americans had for the United States Supreme Court's *Brown v. Board of Education* decision. On May 17, 1954, the court's justices unanimously overturned the "separate but equal" segregated schools legalized in 1896 by the court's *Plessy v. Ferguson* ruling. In *Brown,* the court declared separate inherently unequal and therefore unconstitutional because it provided no equal protection under the law. The justices were correct. The schools for black children were desperately unequal.

In Virginia, there was maniacally ferocious opposition to the *Brown* decision. Led by the Byrd Machine of former governor then U.S. senator Harry F. Byrd Sr., the state legislature adopted a policy that became known as "massive resistance." State laws allowed the governor to shut down any school that dared let black children and white children—American children—read the words "all men are created equal" together in the same schools and classrooms. A handful of schools across Virginia were closed for part of the 1958–59 school year. When a state and a federal court ruled against massive resistance in the winter of 1959, the Commonwealth of Virginia reversed course, striking those laws off the books, and those schools quickly reopened. But massive resistance continued to beat in the hearts of the white

3

community ruling Prince Edward County. Its white supremacy doctrines flowed through their veins. Its virulent racism then bled the county.

White residents and the white board of supervisors in Prince Edward County took matters into their own hands. Ironically, a case from Prince Edward County had been one of the five cases consolidated in *Brown* after African American students went on strike against separate but clearly unequal school conditions at Robert R. Moton High School. Five months after the state abandoned the strategy, the Prince Edward County Board of Supervisors took massive resistance as far as it could, closing schools for five years, only reopening them in 1964 under court order, and then only grudgingly and with minimal funding.

The vast majority of white children had continued their educations in a private, whites-only academy using county tax dollars and state tuition grants. But more than two thousand black students had been left without a formal education as a result of Prince Edward County's school closures. Their lives would never be the same. This book is a first-person account of the attempt to bring healing to that wound four decades later.

The narrative unfolds in Virginia but it is a deeply American story. Prince Edward County's ongoing journey of reconciliation blazes a hopeful and redemptive trail through difficult human terrain, but the signs are clear enough for a divided nation to follow:

We cannot erase the past. The future belongs to someone else. This moment is ours.

1

'God, Please Help Us. We Are Your Children, Too'

Barbara Rose Johns had the audacity to dream. She never saw the night-mare coming.

At first, she dreamed of a new school for black students as good as the school for whites, and she led an April 23, 1951, student strike on behalf of that cause. But the dream became more ambitious. The students of Robert R. Moton High School in Virginia's Prince Edward County soon sought an America where there would be no more white schools and no more black schools. Not in Prince Edward County. Not anywhere in the United States of America. There would just be schools. And there would be no more white children and there would be no more black children. There would just be children. And those children would sit side by side in the classrooms of those schools and learn about the wonderful nation that had brought an end to its apartheid.

Three years later, the U.S. Supreme Court's *Brown* decision made it seem that the vision Johns and her classmates had for their community had come true. But that dream wore black skin and it woke up in the white Southern world of Jim Crow in the 1950s, sixty-five miles west of Richmond, the former capital of the Confederacy.

The dream had no chance. Within days of the *Brown* ruling, the house where the dream found the voice of a sixteen-year-old African American girl, looking at the world through her eyes, was burned to the ground.

Johns's dream had been so innocent and full of faith. A school for black children that was equal to the one for white children. That was all. Instead,

5

TOP: *Robert R. Moton High School, surrounded by the tar paper shacks built to alleviate overcrowding, stood in stark contrast to the white high school a few blocks away.* MIDDLE: *Students prepare for a ninth grade English class at Robert R. Moton High School, circa 1951.* BELOW: *Farmville High School, constructed for whites, was far superior to Robert R. Moton High School. That inequality sparked the student strike by African American students on April 23, 1951. (Photos courtesy of the National Archives and Records Administration, Philadelphia)*

she and her classmates studied hand-me-down textbooks from the white school, in tarpaper classrooms built beside the bursting-at-the-seams Robert R. Moton High School. They went to class in an old school bus, and two teachers taught different classes simultaneously in the school's auditorium.

The school was named for Robert Russa Moton, an African American educator raised in Prince Edward County who succeeded Booker T. Washington as president at Tuskegee Institute.

Johns shared her deep frustrations with a trusted Moton teacher, Inez Davenport, who one day asked her, "Why don't you do something about it?" Johns recalled, in handwritten notes composed years later: "I was surprised by her answer but it didn't occur to me to ask her what she meant. I just slowly turned away, as I felt she had dismissed me with that reply. What could one do about such a situation? I had no idea."

Though nature could transform the landscape around Johns, reawakening colors from the dormant ground, it was powerless to nurture a single bloom in the hearts of white decision-makers.

"I even imagined that a great storm came through and blew down the main building and splattered the shacks to splinters. And out of this wreckage rose this magnificent building and all the students were joyous and even the teachers cried," she remembered.

There were times, she continued, "I just prayed, 'God, please grant us a new school. Please let us have a warm place to stay where we don't have to keep our coats on all day to stay warm. God, please help us. We are your children too.'"

Such thoughts filled her head for months. They were with her as she chopped wood and fed the pigs on the family's twenty-two-acre farm near Darlington Heights, a crossroads some dozen miles from the town of Farmville and its strict segregation.

Johns would let her "imagination run rampant" as she spent many days in her favorite "hangout in the woods on my favorite stump, contemplating it all." A creek flowed nearby under the canopy of trees through which the sun cast patterns of shadow and light.

Jim Crow couldn't find her in the woods. The only crows were those that cawed. The flute-like song of the wood thrush and the occasional call of a red-tailed hawk also punctuated the quiet stillness. The green leaves of summer turned yellow, red, orange, and brown together, and they fell as one all around Barbara Rose Johns. There were no signs on the trees in the woods declaring "red leaves only." Surrounded by the natural seasons of God, the unnatural seasons of man were nowhere to be seen. The stump upon which Johns sat and dreamed was not marked "Colored."

There were no lies in the woods. If someone had taken a Polaroid photograph of Johns at that moment, it would have told the truth.

During the week, Johns's mother, Violet Adele Johns, worked as a clerk for the Navy Department in Washington, D.C., and her father, Robert Melvin Johns, was a farmer, so many of the household responsibilities fell to the teenager. One morning, Johns was so busy making sure her younger siblings got to the school bus stop in time that she forgot her own lunch and had to hurry back home to get it. By the time she returned, the school bus had come and gone "and left me standing there by the roadside waiting to thumb a ride with whomever came by."

After nearly an hour waiting in vain along the country roadside, she saw a school bus coming. The bus was taking the white children to their sparkling two-story Farmville High School, an impressive facility with the added flourish of an inner courtyard.

That bus would go right past the school with the three tarpaper classrooms for black students on its way to the white high school a few blocks away. The bus was half-empty, but the driver did not stop.

Johns was left standing by the side of the road. "Right then and there, I decided indeed something had to be done about the inequality," she wrote. "But I still didn't know what."

All that day, Johns's mind was "whirling" and then, "as I lay in bed that night I prayed for help. That night, whether in a dream or whether I was awake—but I felt awake—a plan began to formulate in my mind. A plan I felt was divinely inspired because I hadn't been able to think of anything until then."

What came next was remarkable for its innocent vigor in the face of the segregation that restricted, isolated, and demeaned Johns.

"We would make signs and I would give a speech stating our dissatisfaction and we would march out of the school and people would hear us and see us and understand our difficulty and would sympathize with our plight and would grant us our new school building and our teachers would be proud and the students would learn more and it would be grand. And we would live happily ever after," she remembered believing, as the dream led her toward its promised land.

For blacks living in Prince Edward County in the 1950s, however, "happily ever after" was a fairytale. To turn her dream into reality, Johns assembled a core group of students from what she described as "the 'creme de la creme'" of Moton High School's student council, among them President John Stokes, his sister, Carrie, and John Watson. They began planning a student strike.

John Stokes recalls that to keep the planning a secret, the students gave their upcoming strike a code name: The Manhattan Project. This was the same name given to the top-secret research and development of the atomic bomb during World War II. Given Prince Edward County's response over the next decade, that code name would prove tragically ironic. On April 23, 1951, the students carried out their strike against the separate and unequal facilities provided for them. The next day Johns and members of her core group walked down Main Street to the county courthouse to make their case directly to county school superintendent Thomas J. McIlwaine.

This was more than four years before Rosa Parks refused to move to the back of a bus in Alabama. The case can thus be made that the two-week student strike represents the birth of the modern civil rights movement—an organized, concerted, and sustained nonviolent protest against segregation. On the U.S. Civil Rights Trail's timeline of significant dates in the civil rights movement, the Johns-led student strike is the first listing.

AMERICA HAS ALWAYS TALKED a good game, but living up to its own founding words was difficult from the moment signatures were applied to the Declaration of Independence on July 4, 1776. "All men are created equal" sounds enlightened enough to illuminate every dark corner of the globe. However, the phrase cast only enough light to ensure that a subset of white males in thirteen former British colonies in North America were considered to be, from the Founding Fathers' point of view, created equal and endowed by their creator with certain unalienable rights.

The Founders' lofty words set our national bar high, but future generations would strive to reach that bar and pull the rest of the country up with them. Johns and her core team were attempting to do just that in April 1951.

In a different Prince Edward County, in a different Virginia, in a different United States of America, in a different world, the students' action would have been celebrated by their hometown, perhaps with a star-spangled parade down Main Street in their honor.

But in that different world, of course, there would have been no tarpaper shack classrooms, no segregation, no Jim Crow, and no ship landing at Jamestown in 1619 with a cargo of African slaves.

The students of Robert R. Moton High School lived in an America with a voracious appetite for segregation, hungry to devour any black person who dared believe America ever truly meant what it said about the equality of all.

Though Johns and her classmates never could have foreseen five years of massive resistance as they went on strike, they knew the world around them was not safe. Johns's dream began to be stalked by the nightmare almost immediately after the legal petition for nonsegregation, drafted by the NAACP attorneys, was signed by the students and their parents.

The students had called African American attorneys Oliver Hill and Spottswood Robinson in Richmond within days of their strike and were advised that the NAACP was no longer fighting to preserve the doctrine of "separate but equal." The new aim was to abolish segregation. So that became the target of Johns, her classmates, and their families in the lawsuit they filed on May 21, 1951, *Davis v. County School Board of Prince Edward County.*

On May 6, a large cross was erected and set ablaze at Robert R. Moton High School. The charred remains were photographed and published by the *Richmond Afro-American* two days later under a bold banner headline. One of the subheads reported that police had termed the cross burning a "prank." Accompanying the news story was a photograph of four students looking at the charred remains.

One of those students was John Stokes, whose memoir, *Students On Strike: Jim Crow, Civil Rights,* Brown *and Me*—penned with Lois Wolfe and Herman J. Viola—was published by National Geographic.

The burned cross was regarded as anything but a "prank" by its targets. When I asked Stokes years later about that May morning in 1951, he deferred answering during our telephone conversation. Instead, he promised to send me words he had composed and set down on paper. "They are from my heart," he told me.

I opened the envelope four days later. On a single sheet of paper, he had written:

> The smoldering cross dwarfed us. As the four of us craned our necks and fixed our eyes on the menacing construction that stood before us, it sent chills through my entire being.
>
> The burning cloths/rags that had been wrapped around the top portion of this heavy wooden structure had now begun to burn out and had fallen to the ground. Those remnants are now curling around the base, withering like snakes and slowly dying out.
>
> The pungent odor is still filled with the aftermath of chemicals and residue that had been used for this ungodly and eerie act. This intense putrid odor penetrated the entire atmosphere around the school. The inner portions of my nostrils burned as I stood there. At that instant, it seemed as if this stench encompassed the entire Universe, a deadness that settled over the entire area, creating a knot that grips the pit of one's stomach that could cause one to regurgitate.
>
> This is not resurrection day. This . . . personifies death.

In the aftermath of the cross burning, he told me, the black community "went into the same type of mode as people who are in a war. We went into protective mode. Not to attack, but for self-defense . . . We knew we had to arm ourselves."

One particularly vivid detail recalled by Stokes was that the fear of reprisal was so widespread and palpable that local stores sold out of shotgun shells. "You could not find any ammunition in Farmville. We had to go to

Lynchburg or Richmond to buy ammunition," he said. That could mean a round-trip journey of approximately a hundred miles.

Potential targets for white retribution included those who had signed the petition that launched the *Davis v. County School Board of Prince Edward County* case. Stokes wrote that he had regarded the burned cross as "an attempt to instill fear into our hearts and minds so that we would remove our names from this petition." Students and parents signed the court petition but attorney Oliver Hill, Stokes told me, made certain that only families who owned their own land affixed their names. That requirement was intended to protect those who signed from the threat of physical harm. Stokes remained a steadfast plaintiff and became part of one of the most momentous U.S. Supreme Court decisions in history.

"As landowners, we had the legal right to protect ourselves and our property. They knew we were armed and that's why there was no bloodshed in Prince Edward County," Stokes said. After the cross was burned, his family never opened the front door at night until it was known who was standing on the front porch. He said the Stokes family always kept a loaded shotgun and a .22 rifle, and whichever male family member was closest to the weapon would pick it up, go out the back door, and walk around the side of the house to see who was there.

But Stokes said the attacks in Prince Edward County were mostly psychological. "They attacked us with words," he told me, referring particularly to the editorials of J. Barrye Wall Sr., publisher of the *Farmville Herald*.

At the time, though, the risk of physical harm could not be ruled out, so Johns's family took action to protect her.

"Barbara Rose Johns disappeared. We, the students, didn't know what had happened to her," Edwilda Allen told those attending an April 23, 2014, commemoration of the student strike, which I covered for the *Farmville Herald*. "We didn't see her. Nobody talked about her. We went back to school and I was one of the ones who was able to finish high school."

Even Johns's closest friends had no idea where she had gone, adding to the black community's sense of unease.

Years would pass before Allen learned that Johns's family had sent her to Alabama to live with her uncle, the minister Vernon Johns, who preceded

Barbara Rose Johns was sixteen when she led the historic student strike at Robert R. Moton High School. The strike is listed first on the U.S. Civil Rights Tour's timeline of significant events in the civil rights movement. (Photo courtesy of Johns family)

Dr. Martin Luther King Jr. as pastor at Dexter Avenue Baptist Church in Montgomery, Alabama. The Reverend Johns preached with a fiery intellect and backed down from no white man.

Thus Barbara Rose Johns graduated from high school in Alabama and never returned to live in Prince Edward after leaving it for her own protection. Her younger sister, Joan, was an adult before she fully understood and appreciated her sister's journey. "Only after I was grown did I realize what a strong, brave, fearless and courageous person Barbara was," Joan Johns Cobbs said during that same public ceremony marking the sixty-third anniversary of the historic student strike.

However, in 1954, when news first spread through Prince Edward County that the U.S. Supreme Court had ruled that segregated schools were unconstitutional, Johns's classmates would have felt their prayers answered, their dream about to come true.

Those feelings were not shared by white segregationists.

In the immediate aftermath of the *Brown* decision, the Johns family home mysteriously burned. The home stood off a country road near Darlington

Heights, making it easy prey for an arsonist. The family was out of town when the home was destroyed but the smoke was still rising when they returned.

"To see it was devastating," Cobbs remembers. "There was nothing left at all. Just ashes."

The local law never made an arrest. "All we know," Cobbs said, "is that it had to be arson. They never investigated or told us what their findings were."

That was how the Johns family was thanked for their role in the landmark *Brown* decision that offered equal protection under the law to all Americans.

2

The 'Civil War' After the Civil War

One aspect of the Civil War clearly did not end in 1865. After the South's surrender, the fate of African Americans continued to be contested. There were no longer armies dressed in blue or gray, but there were dramatically contrary points of view about the integration of African Americans into the full embrace of freedom and equal protection under the law. Did "we, the people," include every person? Or were those words code for a national private "country club"—the United States of White America? The chains of slavery were gone. But the issue of whether the nation was a "white house"—merely a place of systematic, legally enforced domestic servitude for people of color—was still being bitterly contested in the decades after the war.

Full emancipation did not occur when the shooting stopped. Emancipation had been proclaimed, but even eighty-five years later its full realization for African Americans was nowhere in sight.

The root of the Civil War was slavery. Without slavery there would have been no Civil War. The root of massive resistance was white supremacy. Remove it and *Brown* would have integrated Prince Edward schools with ease.

Some have argued the states' rights position for both the Civil War and massive resistance. If so, the Civil War was about a state's right to own slaves and massive resistance was about a state's right to segregate schools. Southern victory in the war would have preserved slavery. The triumph of massive resistance would have preserved segregated schools. Racist objectives motivated the respective conflicts. There was no clearer example of massive resistance's segregationist voice than on the editorial pages at the newspaper where I would eventually make my career.

The ashes of the Johns family home in Prince Edward County were still cooling in 1954 when their white neighbors began joining the Petersburg-based Defenders of State Sovereignty and Individual Liberties, a states' rights organization led by Southside Virginia* leaders who had banded together to oppose *Brown*. (This was about the same time a similar organization, the White Citizens' Council, was formed in Mississippi; chapters spread rapidly across the South.) My future employer at the *Farmville Herald*, J. Barrye Wall Sr., was one of the Defenders' organizers.

The group's application form (preserved in the University of Virginia's Albert and Shirley Small Special Collections Library) did not use words like "courage" and "conviction." There is no noble heroism in its prose, which was for private, not public, consumption and is succinctly to the point. Prospective members were required to sign this statement:

> I am a white, law abiding (sic) citizen of the United States of America, and a resident of the County _____, Virginia. I am not a member of any organization detrimental to the peace and welfare of the U. S. A., nor do I ever intend belonging to such an organization. . . . I believe the segregation of the races is a right of the state government, in the sovereignty of the several states and in the freedom of the individual from government controls . . .

With that solemn pledge, some in Prince Edward County sought membership in an explicitly white-supremacist organization and paid $10 for the privilege of doing so.

To deter infiltrators from the opposing side of the battle over *Brown*, applicants for membership in the Defenders of State Sovereignty and Individual Liberties had to be sponsored by an existing member.

There was no disguise. No carefully contrived overriding states' rights principle is articulated. The focus was entirely racial. The organization's

---

* Southside Virginia refers to the counties south of the James River, which was the first area settled in the colonial period.

members knew exactly why they were fighting. This civil war was about one thing: segregation.

One hundred years earlier, secessionist leaders could have used the same application form, substituting "segregation of the races" with the single word "slavery." In the context of either century, the document reads like an army enlistment paper. A year after the Defenders' founding, it had twenty-eight chapters with a combined twelve thousand members.

No small army. And one that put its troops to use.

THE DEFENDERS OF STATE Sovereignty significantly influenced the development and implementation of Virginia's massive resistance against *Brown,* according to the Virginia Foundation for the Humanities' *Encyclopedia Virginia.*

In 1956 Virginia embraced the anti-*Brown* "Southern Manifesto" that was signed by more than a hundred congressmen, including the entire Virginia delegation. The manifesto was energetically promoted by U.S. Senator Harry F. Byrd Sr., the former Virginia governor who had called earlier that year for massive resistance to school integration. The Virginia General Assembly soon adopted a series of laws, chief among them a statute that would cut state funds for and shut down any public school that dared move toward integration.

Thus in September 1958, Governor J. Lindsay Almond Jr. ordered the closure of nine white schools where desegregation was imminent: Warren County High School in Front Royal, one high school and an elementary school in Charlottesville, and six schools in Norfolk.

However, on January 19, 1959, a federal district court and the Virginia Supreme Court of Appeals both ruled that Virginia's massive resistance laws were unconstitutional and ordered the schools reopened. In response, Almond reversed Virginia's course, directing the General Assembly to wipe the offending laws off the books. All the closed schools had reopened by the end of February.

But in Prince Edward County, whites had already petitioned the all-white local officials to defund the public schools as a defense against *Brown.* That the Commonwealth of Virginia had already abandoned the policy of massive resistance did not deter them. Four months later, Prince Edward County chose to be a law unto itself.

In Front Royal, Charlottesville, and Norfolk, it had taken an order by the governor to close the schools. Prince Edward County—despite the court rulings, despite the governor and the General Assembly having abandoned massive resistance—closed every one of its public schools (and did not reopen them until court-ordered to do so in September 1964).

The Prince Edward County Board of Supervisors' decision was cheered on by the Byrd Machine. Other segregationists across the state and nation added their support. And, despite having repealed its massive resistance laws, the Commonwealth of Virginia allowed state tuition grants to be used by students at the all-white Prince Edward Academy (Prince Edward County would also fund tuition grants for those white students even after its public schools reopened).

The loudest cheers of support came from within the county itself, including from local residents active in the Defenders of State Sovereignty and Individual Liberties.

Lock the school doors, 4,500 white people urged, signing their names to a document that in one short, scalpel-sharp paragraph cut the Declaration of Independence down to a size that fit their own particular definition of life, liberty, and the pursuit of happiness, making their meaning of "all men are created equal" perfectly clear: a white creator had endowed their white lives with certain unalienable white rights.

And so on June 3, 1959, Prince Edward County voted to lock and chain its schools. A private academy for white children seemed to spring up overnight. But a contingency plan for it had begun taking shape in the aftermath of *Brown* as the white power structure maneuvered to ensure that white children would have schools if the county did defund public education. Such action would create an educational vacuum for black children rather than letting both races attend public schools together. Some black children were able to attend school in adjoining counties. Others had to leave Virginia. But most Prince Edward African Americans were left without formal educational opportunities.

IN HINDSIGHT, THE IRONY is inescapable. The same year as *Brown*, the fear of long-range manned Soviet nuclear bombers had prompted the U.S. Air Force, Army, and Navy to create the Continental Air Defense Command. The politicians and commanders in Washington saw the chief threat to the American way of life, liberty, and the pursuit of happiness as Soviet-based. But the new air defense system was blind to events unfolding just a few hours south, in Prince Edward County, where the decay of public education was becoming radioactive to black children.

No mushroom-shaped cloud towered into the sky above the Prince Edward County courthouse in June of 1959. But five years of massive resistance to the U.S. Supreme Court's 1954 *Brown v. Board of Education* ruling would become nuclear in its impact on public education and the lives of those deprived of the learning they should have received.

The decision released its own concussive shock wave. The blast-wind rushed toward the black community. It vaporized black dreams in Farmville. Incinerated black hopes in Prospect. Shattered black futures in Rice and Darlington Heights.

Out in front of the new high school that Prince Edward County had finally built for blacks, the sign would soon read, "School Property. No Trespassing Under Penalty of Law."

The fallout from Prince Edward's actions spread. Casualties were everywhere, the children's wounds growing deeper and wider. Some would spend their lifetimes trying to recover; not all would.

And no one in the Kremlin had had to lift a finger.

MY FUTURE EMPLOYER, J. Barrye Wall Sr., had purchased the *Farmville Herald* in 1921 and remained its publisher and editor/editorial writer until his death at age eighty-seven on October 4, 1985. Wall was not merely a newspaper publisher and business owner in Farmville; by the time he helped organize the Defenders of State Sovereignty in 1954, he was a prominent, influential member of the local white power structure.

At the *Herald*, Wall worked alongside its managing editor, John C. Steck. Nor was Steck merely a local journalist—he was a member of the Prince Edward County Board of Supervisors and was part of the unanimous defunding vote that shut down the public school system in 1959.

In 1960, the *Herald* published a thirty-one page booklet entitled, "The Prince Edward County Virginia Story." In a brief introduction, Wall wrote that he had asked his managing editor to write a "factual account" about the "attempt at forced integration in a locality's public schools."

In the booklet's introduction, Steck described Prince Edward's tragic descent into massive resistance and the destruction of public education as

> essentially the story of a determined, united people and their arduous, but devoted labors, to preserve, by every legal and honorable means, a cherished institution, the education of their children.

This monochromatic worldview was how the *Herald* saw the battle. No mention is made of the determined and united black community and its arduous but devoted labors to provide, by every legal and honorable means, a cherished institution: the education of *their* children.

The *Herald*'s was not an isolated view. The vast majority of whites saw themselves and only themselves as "the citizens" of Prince Edward. "Citizenship" was a distinction whites bestowed upon themselves in towns, counties, and cities across the South. Everyone else, in their eyes, was at best a resident.

Steck continued:

> It is a story of courage. The courage, first of all, of conviction, then of determination, and, not the least, the courage of uncharted invention. To many it has meant consuming sacrifice of time, pleasure, and the normal pursuits as shock and dismay in the spring of 1954 have given way to dauntless action.

Steck's account displayed whites' horror and distress at *Brown,* and their resolute maneuvers to kill its aims. He made certain to add that it is "a story without hate for any man or any race" and without "the slightest trace of deceit, or of threat, or of mistreatment."

The whites-only viewpoint dominated the booklet and concluded with a declaration of "the determination of the citizens of Prince Edward County to give their children an education in the private school system." Steck then solicited readers for "financial support from all who feel that our citizens are waging a worthwhile battle . . ."

Steck was a World War II veteran, discharged as a U.S. Army major after serving in the European theater. At the time Steck wrote the booklet, he was a lieutenant colonel and deputy commander of the 1st Battle Group, 116th Infantry, in the Virginia National Guard. Steck would not have chosen the word "battle" on a whim—he knew front lines when he saw them, and he saw these from the trenches. In the battle over *Brown*, Steck was an active combatant who a year earlier, in his role as a Prince Edward County Supervisor,* had voted to shut down the schools.

NOT ALL OF THE whites who read the *Herald* subscribed to massive resistance. The minutes of the June 23, 1959, Board of Supervisors meeting record that four white residents voiced their concerns:

> The following persons stated to the Board that they had serious doubts that the action in cutting off appropriations for schools and thereby causing the closing of same would be for the best interests of citizens of this County, both white and colored, and urged that further study and consideration be given to the matter in order that conditions detrimental to the County as a whole and particularly to the children of school age might be avoided, viz: Dr. C.G.G. Moss, Mrs. Annie V. Putney, M. Henry Bittinger and Mrs. Grace Putney.

At that same meeting, the Reverend L. Francis Griffin and other African American ministers petitioned the Board to rescind its actions "forfeiting all public education to the children of this community."

Such voices were candlelight trying to shine away a hurricane of darkness. The hurricane won.

How "The Battle of Prince Edward" ended would affect more than the

---

* He would go on to a long tenure on the Board of Supervisors, becoming its vice chairman in 1968 and its chairman in 1972.

fate of that county's people. There would be national repercussions. The final outcome would reinforce battleground sieges going on across the South. Segregation or integration would be fortified. The balance would tip in favor of one side or the other.

The black community endured the wounding of their children in a conflict that would determine whether a public school education free of racial segregation indeed was the constitutional right of every American child.

So it was that legal action renewed over the 1959 school closures. Had the black community in Prince Edward given up their struggle, the fight against segregation and Jim Crow across the South would have been in constant peril. Segregationists in any community could have threatened to shut down public schools unless blacks kept to the separate track proscribed for them by the white powers-that-be. The future of civil rights for African Americans across the nation was at risk. Both sides of the massive resistance fight knew Prince Edward County would heavily influence the outcome of the continuing war.

Virginia's policy of massive resistance and Prince Edward County's use of it to close all public schools were not a continuation of *the* Civil War. They were another chapter in the decades-old "civil war" over extending civil rights to include all Americans.

Nobody was killed in Prince Edward County during the battle over *Brown*. The same cannot be said for other communities. The conflict was real, the encounters bloody. The Southern Poverty Law Center (SPLC) has an entire page on its website dedicated to civil rights "martyrs," from Emmett Till to Martin Luther King Jr.

The "civil war" after the Civil War was all too real.

DR. JILL TITUS TITLED her book *Brown's Battleground* for a reason. This period of U.S. history waged in Prince Edward County decided the fate of the nation-shaping U.S. Supreme Court decision.

The Reverend L. Francis Griffin was pastor of Farmville's First Baptist Church, president of the local NAACP branch, and the acknowledged leader of the black community in Prince Edward County. He held the people together and fought relentlessly for them with wisdom, integrity, and strength. In a 1960 letter* to presidential candidates John F. Kennedy and Richard M. Nixon, Griffin noted the community's massive resistance response to *Brown:*

> This little Virginia community has defied the courts, and violated every principle of democracy. Strong federal intervention is needed to save us from ourselves and guarantee our children a fair chance in an ever-changing world. . . . If you are elected president of this great nation of ours, will you advocate measures to prevent this from happening to other children of the nation? Will you use the powers of this great office to correct this evil that is negatively affecting the lives of approximately 1,400 white and 1,700 Negro children, and by tomorrow could affect the lives of untold numbers of the South?

Three months after Kennedy was sworn in as president—two years into Prince Edward's massive resistance—the Confederate battle flag was raised over South Carolina's capitol dome in commemoration of the centennial of the Civil War—not to spotlight the end of the war, but its beginning. The first shots, not the last.**

PRINCE EDWARD COUNTY'S PUBLIC schools were still tightly shut when Dr. Martin Luther King Jr. visited Farmville on March 28, 1962, accompanied by his friend and right-hand man, the Reverend Ralph D. Abernathy, and by Wyatt Tee Walker, executive director of the Southern Christian Leadership Conference. King spoke at Reverend Griffin's First Baptist Church on Main Street.

In his essay "Fifty-three Hours With Martin Luther King Jr.," Walker remembers Griffin telling him:

---

*   Reported by the *Farmville Herald.*

**   The battle flag was left defiantly atop the dome until a compromise in 2000 moved it to ground level next to the South Carolina State House. The battle flag was finally removed entirely from the grounds on July 10, 2015, in response to furor following the murder of nine African Americans gunned down while worshiping at Emanuel AME Church in Charleston, S.C., by a white supremacist.

"There's a church full of folks waiting to see our 'Moses.'"

I couldn't believe it. This was a farm community. How could [Griffin] have a church full on Wednesday. These people have to be in the fields. It was mid-morning. But they were there. They wanted to see and hear this internationally known leader who was hop-scotching around the South, off the beaten paths, bringing hope and lifting the morale of the plain and simple people of the land. You could see it in their eyes and written all over their faces. "Martin Luther King Jr. is really here in Prince Edward County, Virginia."

The pain, too, was clearly visible.

The SCLC director noted "the obvious lines of weariness and strain" on the face of Reverend Griffin, whom he had known for years. And, as Dr. King subsequently spoke to children in the church's fellowship hall, Walker wrote, "I could not help asking myself—'What kind of nation are we? Three whole years and no public schools.'"

Three years would become five.

King's visit was covered in the March 30 edition of the *Farmville Herald*, which reported that he told those gathered in the church that he was "concerned about your agonizing and suffering moments here in Prince Edward County . . . You have not accepted a half loaf. We all realize that if we are to be free, we cannot sell our birthright of freedom for a mess of segregated pottage."

The suffering, King knew, would continue and he did not hide that fact, according to the newspaper's coverage. But the ultimate goal, he believed, would be worth the pain.

"Stand firm and things will get better . . . Do not despair, do not give up, but just stand firm for what you believe in and people all over the United States will say there are the black people of Prince Edward County who have injected new meaning in the veins of civilization," he said.

Speaking directly to the hammer and nails of massive resistance, King said, "Before you wear the crown of freedom, there is a cross that we must bear." But that Calvary, he assured them, would not be the end of the story.

"Good Friday spells temporary defeat," he said, "but Easter is coming.

Just keep on keeping on and there will be a new day of freedom. When I come back I will see you sitting in integrated schools."

Praising the courageous leadership provided by Griffin, King said the church's pastor "has stood as a giant in this community and has not compromised on any points in his efforts to make the ideals of democracy a reality."

Among those present that day was Griffin's eldest son, L. Francis "Skip" Griffin Jr. "The place was packed. King was King," he told me, also praising the introduction of King by Ralph Abernathy.

"Skip" Griffin was fourteen at the time. He was one of those being denied an education by his own community. More than five decades later, describing that moment, what he recalled most was "the presence of the Spirit" in his father's church.

Griffin knew who King was and why the visit was important. "I had heard about him from my father . . . It had been a long stretch. To have him come, the people needed that. Especially those who were locked out of school. The timing was perfect for the people."

The message Dr. King delivered resonated through his presence: Persevere in a cause that had consequences beyond the borders of their community.

There are two words from King's message that Griffin has never forgotten: "Remain firm. I remember 'Remain firm.'"

Griffin also remembered a woman coming into the sanctuary that Wednesday morning with a large, brown paper bag covering up something that she held in her hands. All eyes were fixed upon her as she walked up the center aisle to the front of the church. Nobody knew what would happen next and Griffin recalled a momentary uneasiness in the church as the woman drew nearer and nearer to King. A few members of the congregation followed closely behind her, just in case, wanting to ensure his safety.

She stopped in front of the pulpit and pulled the paper bag away. The only thing in her hand was the Christian symbol of resurrection after crucifixion. Her only aim was a blessing. She raised the cross, offered those words to King, and returned to her seat.

The preacher's son remembered another detail—Abernathy's introduction of King that morning had been based on Deuteronomy 17:15.

Your leader shall be the chosen one of God.

"The whole (civil rights) movement was based on an updated application of the scriptures," Griffin said. The imagery of King's words that day clearly reflected that spiritual foundation. What remains most vivid to him today is the mood and spirit of that early spring morning in 1962. "The tonal pitch of it was perfect . . . absolutely right," Griffin said. "And how uplifting it felt."

Unlike the anointed kings in Deuteronomy, however, King was leading an army of plowshares against the swords arrayed against them.

BY 1963, THE ONGOING Prince Edward County litigation was making its way slowly through the courts. Attorney General Bobby Kennedy indicated how strongly he felt about the injustice when he proclaimed, at a centennial celebration of the Emancipation Proclamation in Louisville, Kentucky:

> We may observe with much sadness and irony that, outside of Africa, south of the Sahara, where education is still a difficult challenge, the only places on earth not to provide free public education are communist China, North Vietnam, Sarawak, Singapore, British Honduras and Prince Edward County, Virginia.

Meanwhile, the Kennedy Administration surveyed the educational status of the thousand-plus black children in Prince Edward County who were unenrolled. Unsurprisingly, a high number of black children under ten—those who came of school age after the school doors were slammed shut—could not read. In anticipation that the courts would soon order the public schools reopened, the Kennedy Administration sought to recover some of the lost ground. For the 1963–1964 school year, under the guidance of Special Assistant to the Attorney General William vanden Heuvel, the federal government cooordinated a state and local effort that created the "Free Schools in Prince Edward." These were open to any black and white students who chose to attend.

On May 25, 1964, the U.S. Supreme Court's *Griffin v. County School Board of Prince Edward County* decision affirmed the constitutional right of every American child to a free public education in integrated schools. Justice Hugo Black presented the court's majority opinion.[*]

> Closing the Prince Edward County schools while white public schools in all the other counties of Virginia were being maintained denied the petitioners and the class of Negro students they represent the equal protection of the laws guaranteed by the Fourteenth Amendment. . . .
>
> There has been entirely too much deliberation, and not enough speed, in enforcing the constitutional rights which we held in *Brown v. Board of Education, supra,* had been denied Prince Edward County Negro children.

In *Griffin*, the Supreme Court pressed the accelerator.

The justices noted that Prince Edward's closing of its public schools was done "with state acquiescence and cooperation" and declared that "relief needs to be quick and effective. . . . The time for mere 'deliberate speed' has run out."

The justices remanded the case to the District Court "with directions to enter a decree which will guarantee that these petitioners will get the kind of education that is given in the State's public schools."

ON JUNE 17, 1964, U.S. District Court Judge Oren Lewis ordered the Prince Edward County Board of Supervisors to exercise its authority to levy taxes to fund public schools—and to do so within eight days—to ensure the schools opened in the fall.

During a meeting on June 23, 1964, the Board of Supervisors responded to Judge Lewis's order with an appropriation of $189,000 for the rebirth of the county's public school system in the 1964–1965 academic year—much less than the $339,000 funding request.

The *Farmville Herald* quoted the Reverend L. Francis Griffin as describing the appropriation as "hopelessly inadequate." He said the amount of funding "certainly is evidence that an integrated school system is not intended by the supervisors."

---

[*]   *Griffin* was a refiling of the original 1951 *Davis v. County School Board of Prince Edward County*, amended to reflect the 1959 school closings.

Tellingly, the $189,000 funding decision was not the only action by the Board of Supervisors in response to Judge Lewis's decree. The board also voted to appropriate $375,000 for this: "Educational purposes in furtherance of the elementary and secondary education of children in Prince Edward County in private nonsectarian schools. . . ."

A secret decoder was not necessary to understand that those funds were meant for the education of students attending the all-white private Prince Edward Academy.

In essence, during the first year after the court-ordered end to its massive resistance, the county still voted to separately and unequally fund two sets of classrooms, still almost entirely based on race. The courts eventually put an end to the use of county funds for private school tuition grants but, at that moment, what had really changed?

On November 25, 1964, Griffin wrote* in bitter lamentation to William vanden Heuvel:

> The sufferings of the Negro people here are too public to be denied, too severe and long lasting to need detailed reiteration. For generations, our people here had been denied the few rights and pleasures that could make life in this county even minimally bearable. For five years our community was without any public schools, and because of this a generation of our children are permanently crippled and disabled educationally.
>
> For years, we have suffered the ways of peace and sought from the law the justice we have been denied so long. We suffered our children to be destroyed in order that the law might speak. . . .
>
> The law has spoken. We have yet to see it obeyed.

What was clearly visible was the gaping wound in Griffin's people.

There were still those casualties from the fallout of the county's radioactive decision to close schools in the first place. The price paid by the foot soldiers—the children—in the battle over *Brown* looked Griffin in the eye every single day, week after week, month after month, and year after year.

---

*   Letter is in the archives of the American Friends Service Committee.

3

The Click of Cosmic Tumblers

"**Y**ou know what happened here," the woman standing in front of my desk in the second-floor newsroom of the *Farmville Herald* asked. "Don't you?"

I'd been working at the newspaper for less than a year. I had no idea what in the world she could be talking about. But I could tell she hadn't come to complain about a typographical error in our latest edition. Her eyes bore into me with what felt like a blazing mixture of disgust, anger, and accusation.

She was the wife of a professor at Hampden-Sydney College and it was clear she felt my presence on the *Farmville Herald* team was not unlike a sin. Her disappointment in me was palpable.

Little did I know that the question, and its answer, would reshape my life.

She suggested that I go to Longwood College library's rare book room and ask for *They Closed Their Schools* by Bob Smith.

The library was around the corner and just two blocks away on High Street. I sat down in a chair just inside the rare book room—you could not check these books out—and began flipping through the pages. I soon discovered that the seemingly insignificant journey down a tree-shaded sidewalk had taken me to a world I never knew existed—a world that made me feel as if all the bones were slipping out of my body.

Clues to the terrible truth flew from the book like shrapnel from a grenade. Prince Edward County had closed its schools rather than integrate them. I could not believe a community would do that to its own children. The *Farmville Herald* had led the public crusade to do so. I read the name of the man who wrote the pro-massive resistance editorials: He was still the publisher, still wrote all the editorials. I saw him in his office every day. The same family owned the newspaper. I worked for them. I was a member of their team.

When I was hired in June 1979, J. Barrye Wall Sr. was still publisher and editor. His son, William B. "Bill" Wall, was general manager. Bill's oldest son, W. Bidgood "Bid" Wall Jr., was news editor, and Bill's younger son, Steven E. "Steve" Wall, worked in the advertising department; like me, both of the third-generation Walls had graduated from Hampden-Sydney College. They were slightly older but our years on campus overlapped. I had known Steve at college but didn't meet his older brother until I came to work at the *Herald*. I got along well with both Bid and Steve throughout our times together at the newspaper.

The woman who had told me to read *They Closed Their Schools* must have assumed I had knowingly sought employment at the newspaper that had led the charge to massive resistance in Prince Edward County. She might have concluded that I approved. In this case, inferring a shared set of beliefs on race because of someone's last name or where they worked would have been a grave mistake. But I am forever grateful that she made her feelings clear and put that book in my hands.

I could not then or now fathom a community deliberately shutting down its own public school system. As Smith's words shattered my disbelief, my perception of the community around me changed completely. Even the air seemed different.

However, there was no sudden epiphany that my mission in life would be to spend my entire career at the *Farmville Herald* writing and working for racial healing and reconciliation. I was just out of college, trying to get a foothold on life.

AT FIRST, THE YEARS 1959–1964 seemed a lifetime away, ending with the final period after the last word in Smith's book. When one is twenty-two years old, kindergarten and first grade feel like ancient history.

But as the months passed and my thoughts about what happened began to accumulate like leaves beneath a tree, I understood that I was in a continuum. The massive resistance story wasn't over. The story never would be over. The previous chapters had been written, yes. But the story itself continued and I had become part of it, whether I had wanted to be or not. There would be people who'd assume my employment at the *Farmville Herald* signified both my knowledge and approval of the newspaper's editorial opposition to integrated public schools following the *Brown* decision.

Nothing could have been more untrue.

IT WAS YEARS BEFORE I could bring myself to read one of the *Farmville Herald's* pro-massive resistance editorials in its entirety—not until 2012, twenty-seven years after the death of its author, J. Barrye Wall Sr. A friend working on a book project asked me to read a particular editorial over the phone so he could record and later reprint it. The experience left me feeling violated as I heard its ideas being spoken in my own voice. I felt I had betrayed my beliefs simply by speaking those words.

Not until three years later when I started working on this book did I read another of those pro-segregation editorials. Avoiding them during all the earlier editorial writing and strategizing leading up to the *Brown* Scholarships might seem an extreme reaction, but from the bits and pieces of the editorials I had read in various books about Prince Edward County's massive resistance, I knew this policy was best for me. As passionate as I was on this subject, I feared that reading even a few of them would infuriate me into writing an editorial counterattack that could get me fired before I had done everything possible to promote racial healing and reconciliation. I had no fear of expressing my opinion about Prince Edward County's civil rights past, its present and its future. I would come perilously close to being fired from the editorial pages on one occasion. But I stayed away from those large, bound volumes containing a year's worth of *Farmville Herald* editions from the 1950s as if they were the plague.

Then, when I started working on this book, while reading Wall Sr.'s editorial reaction to the *Brown* decision, and particularly his editorials leading up to, and then defending, the Board of Supervisors' vote to shut down public schools by refusing to fund them, I was struck by an immediate, significant impression—there was a detachment from the consequences of pulling the trigger on the words. There was no evident malice or hatred toward African

Americans. In fact, it was as if they did not exist. That was most chilling of all. A May 29, 1959, editorial stated:

> A firm stand was taken by the white taxpayers in 1954, and affirmed in a petition of 4,500 names in 1956 requesting the Board of Supervisors to appropriate no funds for integrated public schools . . . This does not mean abandonment of education. The Prince Edward Education Corporation stands ready to provide education for all white pupils for the coming year. The Corporation will need the unqualified support of Prince Edward white citizens in the troublous days ahead.

Within the editorial, Prince Edward County had no black families, no black children loved by their mothers and fathers.

As the decision to defund public education was being made, a June 5, 1959, editorial again referred to that all-white petition:

> On May 23, 1956, faced again with the prospects of racial integration in the public schools, the people of Prince Edward presented the Board of Supervisors with a petition signed by 4,500 adult white citizens affirming their "conviction that the separation of the races in the public schools of the County is absolutely necessary and do affirm that we abandon public schools and educate our children in some other way if that be necessary to preserve separation of the races in the schools of the County."

The editorial criticized the General Assembly for being "unequal to the task of maintaining the state's position against integration" and said "the board of supervisors, it appears to us, has taken the only practical course, distasteful as it is." The editorial noted that

> the people of Prince Edward launch upon an uncharted sea. Their course is set and we believe they have the will to reach their goal. Faith! In the days ahead many decisions are to be made, some misunderstandings may come, some inconveniences must be borne, disappointments are certain. Only through faith, faith in our leaders, faith in our elected officials,

faith in ourselves, through faith the greatest of problems can be solved.

White faith in white leaders, white faith in white supremacy, in other words, can keep the white world white. A "bleach" of faith to keep the diabolical *Brown* decision in chains.

The rule of law was acceptable, apparently, when it knew its place. As for decisions such as *Brown*—which had the effrontery to want to bring all of the Constitution's "We the People" through the front door rather than the servants entrance—these would be whitewashed in Prince Edward County. A June 19, 1959, editorial declared:

> We agree with the opinion of the Board of Supervisors that Prince Edward has a choice only of integrated public schools, or no public schools. Faced with this choice and mindful of the often expressed opinions and filed petitions from the people of the county, the Board of Supervisors took the only course open to them, refusing to budget funds for public schools. . . .

What the white people want is what white people get and, besides, the white people were forced to close schools, according to the editorial's telling of the story. A May 29, 1959, editorial had already asserted that

> The loss of public schools in the county rests not on those people who have used every means to keep them operating and racially separate but upon those who would destroy them—the Federal Courts, the NAACP and a few misguided Negro citizens.

Reiterating that in Prince Edward County "education is to be provided for all white children, to share and share alike through the support of the people to the Prince Edward School Foundation," the June 19, 1959, editorial concluded by stating:

> The disruption of public education in the County is not the choice nor the desire of a vast majority of its citizens . . . The first steps may have

been forced upon our people now. We must stand resolutely or supinely submit to intolerable conditions."

The "intolerable conditions" were integrated schools.

The complete absence of any mention of the black people and the education of the black children of Prince Edward County in that passage speaks for itself with deafening force. The white powers-that-be had their fingers poised on the nuclear button knowing that the white people with their white children would be safely in the educational fallout shelters the Prince Edward School Foundation would provide. That the equivalent of an educational holocaust was about to be inflicted on the shelterless black community apparently wasn't worth mentioning.

Rabid, foaming at the mouth racism would have been less unsettling to me. Easier, as all stereotypes are for us to believe we understand.

The editorial's matter-of-fact language reflected, in my opinion, the every-day expressions of white supremacy that were as common in communities across America in those days as the loaves of conveniently sliced white bread on grocery store shelves.

J. BARRYE WALL SR. still came to work as publisher and editorial writer every day during my first six years at the paper. I rarely had any meaningful contact with him, but on those occasions when our paths did cross he seemed a kind elderly gentleman.

He had composed and published an editorial against the landmark *Brown* decision four days after the May 17, 1954, decision, describing the Supreme Court's opinion as being "contrary to the history and mores of the South for three hundred years . . ." A moment is all that's needed to realize that for two of those three centuries slavery was the prime social custom and historical feature in the South; Jim Crow shadowed the remaining eighty-nine years.

The eldest son of the Reverend L. Francis Griffin told me that on his deathbed in 1985, Wall sent an emissary to Griffin's widow, Adelaide, expressing Wall's respect for her husband and his apparent uneasiness, as he lay dying, with how massive resistance to *Brown* was carried out in Prince Edward.

As publisher and editorial writer, Wall had the loudest and most powerful public voice—on any issue. The *Herald's* relentless editorial advocacy of resisting public school integration during the 1950s and 1960s, even if it meant closing every school in the county, seems in retrospect to have been the driving force behind the white community's persistent opposition to the *Brown* decision.

Wall had also helped organize the Defenders of State Sovereignty and Individual Liberties. Like me, he had not been content to simply write editorials when it came to a cause about which he was most passionate. The irony is that two editors of the *Farmville Herald* were most passionate about the same subject, but from fiercely opposing points of view.

Wall's deathbed message was conveyed verbally. And the Griffin family did not and does not view it as a straightforward apology for massive resistance. What was conveyed to Adelaide Griffin was Wall's wish that the white power structure "had done things differently," L. Francis "Skip" Griffin Jr. told me in 2015.[*]

The trajectory of J. Barrye Wall Sr.'s mind as he prepared to leave this world is not insignificant.

WHEN I WAS HIRED, the coverage area of the *Farmville Herald's* twice-weekly editions included Prince Edward and the surrounding counties of Amelia, Buckingham, and Cumberland. As a reporter assigned to Buckingham—my beat from 1979 to 1987—I could do nothing about the continued aftershocks from massive resistance. Only the editor of the newspaper could preach editorials of reconciliation and healing, and I saw no chance of ever becoming editor. There were too many Walls working at the paper, two of them just a year or two older than me.

But even early in my career something inside kept telling me to stay. So much so that after leaving an interview for a job with a daily newspaper convinced the position would be offered to me, I called the following day

---

[*] In a September 11, 2015, telephone conversation. I was not able to speak to Mrs. Griffin directly—she was in fragile health—but Skip and his younger brother, Eric, conferred and consulted their mother. Skip had been told by his mother of Wall's message shortly after it was delivered.

and withdrew my application. I didn't understand my feeling of uneasiness at leaving the *Farmville Herald*. I just knew it felt wrong somehow.

After Wall Sr. died on October 4, 1985, there were three changes at the newspaper. His son, William B. "Bill" Wall, became publisher, and Bill's older son, W. Bidgood "Bid" Wall Jr., became editor, and I was named news editor. That position, I felt certain, was the new ceiling of my advancement at the newspaper. Bid, after all, was just a few years older than me. I could never foresee a time when a member of the Wall family would not be editor, at least not in my lifetime.

But Bid left unexpectedly in the spring of 1990, and suddenly I *could* see a time.

Bill became editor and publisher and his younger son, Steven E. Wall, was named general manager and advertising manager. But I was allowed to take the newspaper's editorial writing out for a test drive. Bill explained to readers on May 2, 1990, that I had agreed to contribute editorials and those that reflected my personal opinion would be followed by my initials, JKW. The first of those editorials appeared on May 4 and every editorial in the *Farmville Herald* bore those initials for the next twenty-five years.

In January 1991, I was named editor. Steve, with whom I got along well—as I had with his older brother, Bid—soon became my publisher. Bill moved into the role of publisher emeritus but still came to work every day in his office that adjoined Steve's.

The road that brought me back to Prince Edward County—and then kept me there—now made complete sense. In addition to control over front-page news coverage, the newspaper's editorial page pulpit was somehow mine.

I felt a call.

I would stay in that small college town in rural Virginia and join my voice with other voices, join my heart with other hearts, and my hands with other hands. As editor my voice would speak loudly and have a strong influence on the community and the direction it took—the impact of J. Barrye Wall Sr.'s editorials had clearly proved that.

I led the news team for thirty years and was fortunate to work with a series of hard-working, self-motivated, good-hearted individuals. They made my job easier. The three colleagues with whom I served the longest—Rob

Chapman, Tana Knott, and Marge Swayne—proved themselves to be out-
standing journalists across the combined ninety-plus years that our bylines
appeared together. They were there during the *Brown* Scholarship crusade
and I could always depend upon their contributions to the newspaper.

EDITORIALLY, MY INVOLVEMENT WITH massive resistance began to heat up
in 1993. The county was then planning to sell the former Robert R. Moton
High School, where Barbara Rose Johns, John Stokes, and their classmates
had made history. The county stated its intention to use the proceeds from
the sale to invest in an addition at the county's middle school. Any developer purchasing the Moton property would, of course, tear down the old
school building to make room for new construction. Many people thought
a fast-food restaurant would be the likeliest outcome.

But there were some in the community who thought that if the building were out of sight, the massive resistance history would eventually slip
out of mind. Some began to call for preserving the school and converting
it into a civil rights museum.

The Martha E. Forrester Council of Women was leading the fight to prevent the building's destruction. I lent my voice to the cause of those African
American women. The November 24, 1993, editorial titled "Prince Edward
County Can Make History By Preserving The Moton-Branch School," was
the beginning of my operating overtly as a change agent or, as John Stokes
would later describe it, "a social engineer." The issue provided me with an
important opportunity to "preach." I wrote:

> A museum would be a positive way to preserve both the building
> and the community's role in the historic Supreme Court decision. Prince
> Edward's role in the case is something the community can be proud of
> . . . The museum could highlight the positive achievement of community
> members who figured so prominently in the historic *Brown v. Board* case.
> The people of Prince Edward should take credit for that.
>
> And, should blacks and whites join hands to create a museum out of
> the Moton-Branch School, it would be a healing act of affirmation in the
> people of Prince Edward County. The museum would be a monument to

our growth as people. This is an opportunity which should not be missed.

There is a rich and significant history here that has never been appropriately recognized or appreciated by the county. A museum at the school is not only appropriate, it is also necessary.

The editorial raised a few eyebrows, which needed raising. Though others would have to wait and see, I knew my course was set. Coverage to preserve the building and convert it into a civil rights museum would be given steady and prominent placement on the front page, in addition to editorial support.

I had been given a copy of the 1959 John Steck-authored booklet by my employers at the *Herald* shortly after I learned about the paper's role in massive resistance. Steck was already deceased. If the goal was indoctrination, the attempt to persuade a young man to embrace the ideology of "The Prince Edward County Virginia Story" failed.

In the years to come, I never asked permission to write an editorial on a particular subject, and I never told the Walls what the next editorial would be about. I wrote the editorials and pasted them up on the layout page—in the old days before computer pagination—in the first-floor production room. If Bill or Steve saw them before the paper went to press, they knew what was coming. Otherwise, no, they did not.

On a February day in 1995, the news department received a phone call from Richmond telling us that Prince Edward County was resisting an attempt by the state to declare the former Robert R. Moton High School a historic landmark—the designation might jeopardize the county's plans to sell the building. I stopped what I was doing and wrote:

> If we're going to tear down the former R. R. Moton High School—now Farmville Elementary—let's go ahead and tear down Independence Hall, too, and dump the Liberty Bell in the river. Let's use the oldest extant copy of the Declaration of Independence to make a paper airplane and throw it off the Washington Monument, which will also be torn down and replaced by a fast-food restaurant.

The editorial, published on February 15 and titled "Shall We Tear Down America?," argued that

> America tends to trivialize virtually everything, from marriage to life itself, so that tearing down one of just five *Brown v. Board* school sites in the nation may be within our distorted sense of values.
>
> Seem far-fetched? Well, in fact, we do have Prince Edward's board of supervisors deciding, not in open session but over the phone, to step in and delay consideration of this supremely historical school building for inclusion on the Virginia Landmarks Register and the National Register of Historic Places.
>
> That process is now stopped dead in its tracks . . . one County official has even pointed out that if the school is torn down the property's value would increase dramatically because the land could be used commercially. Prince Edward doesn't need the value of the property to increase. The building is already priceless. History—and I can't believe I feel compelled to make this point—is more important than hamburgers.

After fourteen more paragraphs of vehemence, I concluded that editorial with these words: "We're not talking about a pile of bricks. We're talking about the soul of America."

My passion did not go down well with Bill Wall. The son of the late J. Barrye Wall Sr. came upstairs to my office and said he wanted me to "tone it down." I refused to do so. There was no way I was going to change a word. Once I let Bill, or anybody, begin to slice away a single phrase, I feared, cutting paragraphs would follow, and the meaning and the power of the editorial would be diluted beyond recognition.

From that point on, Bill began to pay more attention to my editorials before they went to press. His son, Steve, the publisher, never interfered with my editorializing. I never once had a confrontation with him. I had the occasional discussion on various subjects with Steve, who also sold ads for the paper, but never with swords drawn. I cannot recall even a single instance of Steve expressing displeasure over one of my editorials—on any subject. Ours was an easy relationship.

Speaking of my editorial writing in 1997, Steve told *They Closed Their Schools* author, R. C. "Bob" Smith, "People in the street ask me why he said what he said today and I say it's his business to say what he thinks. If I tell him what to say, I might as well do the job myself." Smith included the quote in his *Virginia Quarterly Review* piece, "Prince Edward County: Revisited And Revitalized."

In the summer of 1997, I was standing at a reception in the Robert Russa Moton Museum with former Fifth District Congressman, L. F. Payne Jr. The two of us were being honored for our support of the museum.

There had been discussions around the country, thanks to President Bill Clinton, about a national apology for slavery. Speaking in the same auditorium where Barbara Rose Johns's speech launched the modern civil rights movement forty-six years earlier, I used the occasion to make my own apology:

> A tidal wave of history began breaking on the shores of this nation with the arrival in Virginia in 1619 of the first Dutch ship filled with Africans. They were sold as slaves in a New World that really wasn't so new after all. And the tidal wave kept breaking. We've been swimming in it and now, thank God, out of it, ever since.
>
> People wonder—among them President Clinton and members of Congress—if it would be a good thing for America to apologize for slavery. Of course it would be a good thing. An apology for slavery and all of the invisible chains that followed. I see nothing to debate. And I would love to see Virginia take this high ground first because those ships of slaves first came to our state's low ground.
>
> Some say an apology needlessly digs up the past and, besides, we've made so much progress. But we must understand that slavery isn't just about the past. It's still influencing our present. It will influence our tomorrows. We're still dealing with the repercussions. The lingering effects of slavery aren't dusty skeletons in a distant closet. Those bones have flesh and blood . . .
>
> Certainly, an apology would have great symbolic value but I also believe it would provide an impetus for black Americans and white Americans to look each other more closely in the eye, and in the heart. It would slip

beneath the veneer and into our roots. We would grow closer together as a people. A national apology could spark millions of smaller but no less important moments of peace between individuals all over this land. And I hope and I pray that this is one of them because I don't want to wait for the President or for Congress to say I'm sorry.

As I spoke, I was looking at the faces before me. Many eyes were welling up with tears. The audience included men and women who had been locked out of school by massive resistance and denied an education only because they were black. Looking as many people in the eye as I could, and using their names to make the moment as personal as possible, I told them,

I am terribly angry, terribly saddened, and terribly ashamed of slavery, of segregation, and all that was done in their name. And I want to say tonight to my brothers and sisters, to my friends, to Lacy, Vera, Chuckie, Thomas, Tony, to Grace, that I am—truly—very, very sorry.

[Let us celebrate] our colors and our cultures, not be separated by them. Let's make a song, not a shout, of these notes and join our voices in melody, in harmony. Let us also have a dream and let's live it with our hearts and our minds and our eyes wide open.

No more tidal waves. No more tides. Just us, standing on the shore. Standing here. Tonight. Together. This is a reception. Then let us be receivers. Let us receive each other."

And we did.

The response among those listening was powerful. I was asked to print what I had said in the *Farmville Herald*. The words appeared on the editorial pages of our June 27, 1997, edition as a by-lined op-ed, rather than the editorial—that is how I got it published.

I KEPT PUSHING THE edge of the editorial envelope until I nearly pushed myself out of the *Farmville Herald*. On Easter Monday of 2001, an editorial was removed in its entirety before it could be printed. The editorial focused on the fiftieth anniversary of the historic student strike by the students of

Robert R. Moton High School on April 23, 1951. The words echoed some of the themes and imagery I'd used in the 1995 editorial that Bill had wanted me to tone down. This time, he wanted every sentence, every paragraph, every word removed. Or else.

Among those words were these:

Since 1776, America has struggled to live up to words it felt were important enough to carve on monuments in our nation's capital or guard in a nuclear-bomb-proof chamber below the streets of Washington, D.C. Founding words safe from the threat of nuclear attack, but terribly vulnerable to our simply turning away from them," I had written.

Preserving parchment means nothing without living the words out on the pavement . . . The events of April 23, 1951, helped transform this nation into a land where words like life, liberty, and the pursuit of happiness weren't simply icing on a cake behind a pane of glass on the other side of a door that was locked to some people because of the color of their skin. . . .

As a second-grader in 1964 singing 'America, The Beautiful' and pledging allegiance every morning, I had no idea that my education, and the education of every child in every community in America, was a right guaranteed by a U.S. Supreme Court decision based solely on a case from Prince Edward—*Griffin v. County School Board of Prince Edward,* which made *Brown v. Board of Education* live up to its words—where I had been born.

I sang, asking God to shed His grace on America and to 'crown our good with brotherhood, from sea to shining sea,' without any notion of the courage and strength needed—and still needed—to make America beautiful for all its citizens; or that if it isn't beautiful for all its citizens it isn't America, the beautiful.

I recited the words "with liberty and justice for all," and did not know I was pledging allegiance to something that was a fact for me because I was white but was often fiction—north, south, east and west—to anybody else because they weren't.

But America is more beautiful today, and there is more liberty and justice for more people, because of the mirror Prince Edward students held up to America 50 years ago.

I believed every word with every fiber of my being.

Steve was out of town when Bill called me into his office. He lectured me, concerned that I was needlessly and perhaps hurtfully stirring things up. He told me if I did not pull the editorial entirely then they would find someone else to write editorials. I was deeply shaken and pulled the editorial. I felt certain he would pull it himself if I refused.

It was a crisis moment. Had I betrayed my deepest beliefs by giving in? Should I have resigned on the spot, or made Bill fire me? I feared my "ministry" in Prince Edward County was over, whether I stayed or not. If I was no longer able to preach from my heart, there was no point in my being there.

I debated whether to resign. After praying about it, I decided that leaving the newspaper would achieve nothing. In fact, it would likely hurt the community. The reason for my resignation would certainly become known—J. Barrye Wall Sr.'s son forced Woodley to pull the editorial—and that might amplify old echoes. Crucially, too, I had no idea what kind of editorial "voice" might take my place, but I doubted it would be like mine. Bill might start writing the editorials and I didn't want that to happen. The call I heard was: *Remain.* I would bide my time and begin to push toward the edge of the envelope all over again.

But I felt the loss of those words. I submitted the editorial to three daily newspapers in the region. Each printed it. (Fourteen years later, as my journalism career was coming to its end in May 2015 after the *Herald* was sold, I remembered there was unfinished business. I tracked down that editorial and published it in the *Farmville Herald.* Yes, I am that stubborn.)

BILL WALL AND I knocked heads a few times, but if there are no bumps in his or her way, an editor is on the wrong path, an easy one already smoothed by others. I was making my own way. A framed print hung on the wall beside my desk at the newspaper where I worked for thirty-six years.

DO NOT GO WHERE THE PATH MAY LEAD. GO INSTEAD
WHERE THERE IS NO PATH AND LEAVE A TRAIL.

The bottom line of my professional experience with the Wall family is gratitude for the opportunity and longevity of my editorship. Furthermore, their ownership over the entire twenty-five years of my editorial-writing career adds greater depth and meaning to everything written and done in the *Herald* on behalf of racial healing and reconciliation. The identical words and deeds would not have had the same resonance under different ownership. They would have been accompanied by this qualifier: "Oh, yes, but the Walls don't own the newspaper anymore."

The minutes of the June 23, 1959, Prince Edward County Board of Supervisors meeting list the names of twelve people who publicly endorsed the decision to close schools rather than proceed with integration. One of them was W. B. Wall—Bill. I went through the newspaper's microfilm archives to be certain of that speaker's identity.

The *Farmville Herald's* coverage of that meeting in its June 26, 1959, edition was headlined "12 Endorse, 4 Question Fund Cut-Off At Budget Hearing." The story contains this paragraph:

> William B. Wall, also of Farmville, told the board he felt it "would be perfectly ridiculous to appropriate funds for education of any sort. We'd be in an identical situation with Norfolk. If school funds come into the treasury we'd be ordered to integrate, and we'd be forced to do it, not by the 101st Airborne Division, but by State Troopers at the orders of the state government."

I first read these minutes and the *Farmville Herald's* reporting of that meeting while writing this book. Doing so deepened my appreciation of the years I was able to preach from the editorial page's pulpit and the words I was free to print in my "sermons." If Bill had really wanted to silence me, I reflected, he could have. He surely could have imposed policies to impede or muzzle me, such as pre-approval of editorial topics, with some topics off-limits entirely. He never did. Nor, of course, did Steve.

Even after Bill's ultimatum on Easter Monday in 2001 I never once told him or Steve what the next issue's editorial would be about. Nor did they ever ask. But they did begin receiving an advance copy of every issue's editorial pages from production staff—a very normal thing to do—so they knew what was coming.

Though anxiety that he might do so again—with dire consequences—was my constant companion, Bill never ordered another editorial to be removed or changed by even a single sentence or word. And like Steve, he favored creation of the *Brown* Scholarships.

I have a hard time believing that the man who told the Board of Supervisors it "would be perfectly ridiculous to appropriate funds for education of any sort" would then challenge my "ministry" on the editorial pages only twice in a quarter century. But that is what happened.

Because of our varying backgrounds and upbringing, none of us begin life's journey at the same place, and so none of our journeys are the same. The topography of our inner landscapes—the way our environment and experiences shape our beliefs—can be wildly different. What matters most is how far one is able to go beyond his or her initial personal terrain to find common ground with others.

Bill Wall came to work full-time at his father's newspaper in 1954, the year of *Brown*, the year his father helped to found the Defenders of State Sovereignty and Individual Liberties. Had the circumstances of our births been different, our roles might have been reversed. Bill might have been me. I might have been him. The editorial freedom he permitted Steve to allow me speaks well of his journey, and hopefully for us all.

As for Steve, I will be forever grateful for that complete and inherently supportive freedom on the editorial page. No publisher could give an editorialist a freer hand than he gave me.

THERE IS A LETTER that I wish had not been lost among the pack-rat clutter of my office: W. Bidgood Wall Jr., whose sudden departure as editor opened the door for me to begin writing editorials in 1990, sent me a telling note in the mid-2000s. Bid knew I was a Beatles fanatic and revered John Lennon. It had been Bid, then news editor, who told me of John Lennon's murder.

"I didn't think I'd see you today," he said, before breaking the news on the morning of December 9, 1980.

His note two decades later came out of the blue. I hadn't heard from him in the years since he left. I cannot remember the precise wording of his message, but I cannot forget the gist—that my years as editor of the *Herald* were in tune with Lennon's spirit of imagining all the people living together in peace. His message was clear to me, and I deeply appreciated his expression of those feelings.

In 2003, my "ministry" for healing and reconciliation would turn into a "crusade" for reparations in the form of scholarships.

Virginia Commonwealth University emeritus professor Edward H. Peeples reflected on the irony of the scholarship proposal's origin—the editor of the *Farmville Herald*.

"The cosmic tumblers," he told me, "are clicking into place."

They were.

4

Balm for Gilead

I wasn't prepared for the depth of John Stokes's response when I called in early 2003 and told him about the scholarship idea.

As student council president at Robert R. Moton High School, Stokes had been among the first people Barbara Rose Johns enlisted to organize the historic 1951 student strike. That strike played a part in the 1954 triumph of *Brown v. Board of Education*. But then in 1959, he had to suffer the pain of Prince Edward County shutting down its public school system in defiance of *Brown*.

By 1959 Stokes no longer lived in Prince Edward County. He served two years in the U.S. Army after graduating from Moton, and then after his military discharge he earned a degree from Virginia State University. But Prince Edward County remained full of people he knew and loved. Their wounding by massive resistance hurt him in ways I couldn't even imagine.

The scholarship concept came to me on my thirty-five-mile drive from adjacent Appomattox County to my office at the *Farmville Herald*, which gave me time to assemble my thoughts each day. I had plenty to think about that winter morning in 2003 as I drove past the nearby McLean House, where Robert E. Lee surrendered to Ulysses S. Grant—in Appomattox Courthouse National Historical Park.

That morning I was contemplating twin vines whose fruit held the promise of healing communion. The Virginia General Assembly was considering an apology for massive resistance—a resolution of "profound regret" over the

1959–1964 school closings in Prince Edward County and the state's role in those closings. The resolution, I was deeply moved to hear, was heading toward passage.

Meanwhile, the Prince Edward County School Board—sparked by the suggestion of high school Latin teacher Linwood Davis—had begun discussing presenting honorary high school degrees to those prevented by the school closings from earning real diplomas.

There was true goodness in both the resolution of profound regret and the honorary diplomas; these were genuine actions to offer healing and reconciliation. But with regard to the state, I found myself thinking that if one is going to apologize for massive resistance, it would be far better to say, "I am sorry and this is what I intend to do about it."

After all, this would be no apology for something in Virginia's deep past that caused suffering for people who had long since passed from the face of the Earth. The children locked out of public schools for those five long years were by this time in their fifties and sixties. They walked the same sidewalks I did, drove down the same streets, shopped in the same stores, ate in the same restaurants. Some of us had worked together in the 1990s to save the former Robert R. Moton High School from the wrecking ball; the building was subsequently declared a National Historic Landmark.

The resolution of profound regret and honorary diplomas would go as far as they could to ameliorate the school closings. But neither would give back what had been stolen by massive resistance: educational opportunity. That act of reparation had never been attempted.

As I approached the Prince Edward County line that morning, the resolution and the honorary degrees merged in my mind. In that instant, an entire concept for state-funded scholarships for the casualties of massive resistance materialized: from GED, to community college, to a four-year degree and, if desired, sequentially in a complete journey.

Give back what was stolen—the opportunity to earn real diplomas. An act of reparation is an attempt to repair the harm done to someone. State-funded scholarships would be a means to do so, to the best of our ability so many years after the harm had been done.

We could not go back in time, we could not rewrite history—nor should anyone try. But we could write with our deeds a new history of the greatest possible healing.

I COULD NOT WAIT to get to my office to start acting on the new idea, and I have no idea how I avoided a speeding ticket. Before lunch I had a commitment from House of Delegates member Viola Baskerville and State Senator Benjamin Lambert to introduce the necessary legislation. Mid-February was far too late to inject such a proposal into the 2003 session, they told me. Next year would do fine; 2004 would mark the fiftieth anniversary of the *Brown* decision.

I had never met either of these two legislators. I chose Baskerville because of her deep involvement with the resolution of profound regret then moving through the General Assembly. She seemed a natural fit for what was, to my mind, the next logical legislative step—follow the apology with something to repair the harm. Both Baskerville and Lambert were African American legislators from the Richmond area. They were Democrats in a General Assembly controlled in both houses by the Republican Party. Interestingly, Lambert, the Senate patron of my scholarship idea, was married to one of Barbara Johns's cousins, a fact I did not know until he told me that morning.

As soon as I had Delegate Baskerville's commitment, there was one telephone call I had to make. I just hoped that John Stokes would be home. My fingers were trembling with excitement as I punched the numbers on the touchtone phone to dial his home in a Washington suburb of Maryland on February 18, 2003. My heart was pounding as the phone rang. And then Stokes answered. And I laid out the idea.

His response changed the landscape of my life.

"It's tear-jerking . . . A dream come true, an unimaginable dream . . .," said Stokes, who began a lifelong career in education with a teaching position in the public school system of Baltimore, Maryland, before retiring there as a principal. As an educator, Stokes's understanding of the human wound created by massive resistance would have deepened with each passing year. His understanding of what this scholarship program could mean was profound.

"We've been praying this would happen," he said. "I didn't think I'd see it in my lifetime . . . I'm just overwhelmed . . . I'm very overwhelmed by it . . . I would like to be there. Thank God for you. Thank God for your presence."

He asked me to go to the final two verses of the eighth chapter of the book of the prophet Jeremiah. I reached for *The New English Bible* which belonged to my late grandmother and was on the bookshelf behind my desk. I began flipping the pages.

Read the words, Stokes said. My eyes read and my heart was overwhelmed by this:

> *Harvest is past, summer is over,*
> *And we are not saved.*
> *I am wounded at the sight of my people's wound:*

The author, right, and John Stokes arm-in-arm in front of the Prince Edward County Courthouse following the fiftieth anniversary commemoration of the 1951 student strike at Robert R. Moton High School. Stokes had been one of the student leaders enlisted by Barbara Rose Johns to help plan the protest against separate and unequal conditions at the school. (Photo by Mildred Stokes)

I go like a mourner, overcome by horror.
Is there no balm in Gilead,
no physician there?
Why has no new skin grown over their wound?

State-funded scholarships, Stokes told me, would make the dream of reaping the harvest, turned into nightmare by the county's decision to shut down its public schools, possible.

The seeds had been sown, he said, "then the seed was taken out of the ground . . . You're planting those seeds again."

Throughout the morning, adrenaline had been surging through me. I felt almost intoxicated. With his words and those of Jeremiah, Stokes took me beyond exhilaration. Excitement was the wrong emotion. Sober, total commitment was necessary. I could not simply write an editorial calling for the Commonwealth of Virginia to create these scholarships. The call I felt at that moment was to give myself to them entirely and without ceasing.

Rightly or wrongly, I believed Stokes was telling me that I was the physician who would soothe the wound of his people in Prince Edward County. Later, as I wrote this book, I hesitated to share this feeling lest it be read as supreme hubris or a "Messiah complex."

But Stokes had taken me to a place I could never have found alone. This was no egotistical mindset. It was a moment of awesome—almost terrifying—grace. Something far greater than myself overwhelmed me, and it left an impression.

The feeling of personal responsibility embedded within me because of Stokes's reaction to the scholarship possibility must be understood. It informed and compelled my every step for the next sixteen months. This was despite a recurring question that was my constant companion as I began traveling down the twisting corridors of power: Who, me?

A MONTH PASSED BEFORE I published a single word about the scholarship idea, four weeks of working behind the scenes to ensure the idea had a real chance of passage in the legislature.

I initially called it the Prince Edward County Scholars Fund. Stokes, noting there were also whites who had been unable to continue their education after the five-year lapse, heartily approved. "Prince Edward County is a color-blind name," he observed, and "will not segregate anyone."

Also, common sense suggested that massive resistance had generational consequences, and because I knew that going back to school at the age of sixty might not work for many, it seemed logical that the program should accommodate children and grandchildren, too.

In fact, according to the calculations of Virginia Commonwealth University professor emeritus Edward H. Peeples, the school closings in Prince Edward County resulted in 2,202 black youths receiving little or no formal public education during their lifetimes. There were other casualties, as well. Dr. Peeples concluded that 1,064 children were raised in homes by parents to whom formal education was denied. And those children became parents to 883 children, the chains around school doors still locked, in varying degrees, around their family tree. And to Stokes's point about there being white casualties, too, Peeples's 2003 study concluded that 258 white youths were directly affected by the school closures.

As Dr. Jill Ogline Titus, author of *Brown's Battleground: Students, Segregationists, and the Struggle for Justice in Prince Edward County, Virginia,* wrote in a letter to William J. Howell, speaker of the Virginia House of Delegates, in 2014:

> All these stories point to the lingering effects of the school closings in Prince Edward County. Despite their best efforts to the contrary, parents who are plagued by illiteracy and chronic insecurity pass aspects of these handicaps on to their children. Parents who are illiterate or poorly educated don't have the skills necessary to help their children with homework, be advocates for their interests within an educational setting, or help them plan for higher education.
>
> Nor can they make daily reading a part of their children's home life, an activity that is so important to a child's cognitive development that the American Association of Pediatrics now encourages pediatricians to talk with parents about reading with their child at every doctor's appointment.
>
> Both love of learning and educational handicaps are frequently passed

from generation to generation and while some children who are blessed with exceptional intelligence or significant outside support can overcome the obstacles, others are not so fortunate. Though not in so direct a fashion as their parents', their own lives have also been constrained by the legacy of massive resistance. . . .

HELPING TO HEAL THE wounds of massive resistance was why I'd decided to stay at the *Farmville Herald* after the editor's pulpit was unexpectedly vacated, giving me an opportunity in 1990 that I never thought would cross my path. That 1994 letter I mentioned in the Preface, from the legendary civil rights attorney Oliver Hill, had confirmed my sense of calling. But until the morning of February 18, 2003, anything as powerful as giving back the educational opportunity that was stolen in June of 1959 was beyond my wildest dreams.

I was not the only one dreaming.

On a slightly overcast afternoon in April 2003, I was sitting in my office at the *Herald* when I heard footsteps in the stairwell. Members of the public were always climbing those stairs, bringing church announcements, a letter to the editor, news releases—you name it. Footsteps were part of our daily soundtrack, never calling particular attention to themselves. But something this day caught my attention. I left the rest of a sentence unfinished. The footsteps paused at the top of the stairs.

Then John Hurt walked through the door.

And a part of John Hurt never left. By the time I heard his footsteps return down the stairs, I felt as if I had known Hurt all of my life.

When Prince Edward County closed its public schools in 1959, Hurt had just completed the first grade. Massive resistance created a crater in Hurt's life that he had never been able to fill. He was one of the 2,202 black students left without a formal education.

"I just wanted to say thank you," Hurt told me, "for what you're doing."

I have never met anyone in life more determined to succeed than John Hurt. The man was working two jobs—for the Virginia Department of Transportation by day and by night for the Buffalo Shook Company, which manufactured pallets.

This is what Prince Edward County had done to itself in 1959: it had deprived itself of the full impact John Hurt could have made on the community. Hurt was making contributions to the world he and I shared. No question. But I couldn't help thinking about what had been lost. Combine Hurt's incredible work ethic, astonishing will, and perseverance with a complete education, and the community would have benefitted in so many ways from this one human being. But he and 2,201 others were denied the chance to develop and contribute the full measures of themselves. Hurt, who was being tutored in reading, assured me he would certainly embrace the scholarship program if given the chance.

This man whose last name personified the wound to John Stokes's people made massive resistance personal for me. He gave the scholarship crusade a single life for which I would fight. What I didn't know then—and what he would tell me twelve years later—is that on that cloudy April day in 2003 when we first met, John Hurt, fifty-two years old, could barely write his name.

The indomitable spirit of John Hurt is one reason I never use the word "victim" to describe the children wounded by massive resistance. John Hurt is no victim; he is a casualty from that "civil war" after the Civil War, a wounded hero who soldiered on.

Hurt, like so many black men and women, refused to accept white Prince Edward County's valuation of his worth, as defined by the use of massive resistance to separate the races at the cost of an entire public school system.

We would rather lock every door to every classroom, the white community told the black, and destroy public education entirely, than allow our children to go to school with yours. And so they'd locked John Hurt out of school. But he'd never let them throw away the key to his life.

5

'I'll Fight With You on This'

Virginia Governor Mark Warner topped my recruitment list for allies in the scholarship crusade. With the governor by our side, how could we fail? In late March 2003 I contacted his press secretary, Ellen Qualls, and told her I had an idea to discuss with the governor. I'd had good experiences with Qualls, a top professional I greatly respected, and with Warner. I expected to hear from the governor, and I did.

Warner called me at the *Farmville Herald* on April 2, and I introduced him to my state scholarship proposal for the casualties of massive resistance. "The thought is an interesting one," he responded, though he did express a concern that such a scholarship fund "opens up the issue of reparations."

The issue of reparations didn't bother me. Virginia *should* try to repair the harm done by massive resistance, but I understood that for many people the word raised red flags. Reparations came with a price tag.

"Virginia's broke," the governor told me matter-of-factly. But Warner had no concern about scholarships "from moral standpoints."

The state's disastrous financial condition was understandably a major concern for the commonwealth's chief executive. Revenues had fallen and the situation was exacerbated by fulfillment of the "No Car Tax" campaign promise of his predecessor, Republican James S. Gilmore. The measure required state reimbursement to local governments for lost personal property tax revenue as the levy was phased out.

Warner took office in January 2002 and had barely gotten the gubernatorial seat warm when he learned there was a budget shortfall of nearly $4 billion, which would grow to approximately $6 billion.

Facing the state's most dire financial crisis in decades, Warner and the General Assembly had to do something profound to restore stability after a fiscal debacle not of his administration's making. Warner was looking toward a 2004 session of the General Assembly during which he would call for a creative, multifaceted plan that combined tax cuts in some categories and increases in others. Winning passage of the plan would be difficult as the Democratic governor dealt with a bicameral legislature controlled by Republicans. Even the GOP was at odds with itself over the best means of addressing the budget crisis. The bitter political conflict would eventually threaten to shut down state government. The seriousness of the economic crisis could not be overstated.

I was certain Warner embraced the scholarship program proposal's moral imperative. That was the man I knew. However, encouraging his head to follow his heart might become difficult, particularly with grave fiscal issues at stake.

"Get me some stuff and we'll talk again," he promised, adding, "It's frankly a little bit of a challenge . . . as worthy as the cause is."

My emotions were mixed. I was grateful for Qualls's follow-through and the governor's ear. But I had been hoping, perhaps naively, that he'd be totally committed from the outset.

I FIRST MET WARNER in June of 1999 when he was chief executive officer of Columbia Capital Corporation and visiting localities across the state to discuss venture capital possibilities and how they might help area economic development. I was impressed by his intelligence and approachability.

Four months later I caught a glimpse of the inner man, and that reflection held me. We shared a private moment after Warner gave the keynote talk for a five-day symposium at Hampden-Sydney College focusing on the legacy of Prince Edward County's civil rights history. The symposium was breaking new ground in the county where many whites wanted massive resistance to be swept under a large rug. Never had such a comprehensive public event focused on the community's civil rights legacy and its continued reverberations.

Warner and I spoke backstage about what massive resistance had done to those locked out of school for five years. He shook his head and wondered, almost in a whisper, what he could do to help. The depth of his bewildered sincerity made a lasting impression.

Clearly, Warner had no idea: such was the magnitude of the history. Equally evident was the fact that I had nothing to suggest to him. But his struggle seemed so genuine that I felt I had to offer encouragement. Someday, I told him, I knew he would do something—the most pathetically vague optimism possible. Nevertheless, I had a feeling that somehow, someday, he would. He was a man of great means and political possibilities. He'd lost the U.S. Senate race to incumbent Republican John Warner in 1996 by an unexpectedly respectable 52–47 percent. Who knew what the future might hold?

Two years later, during the late-summer of 2001 run-up to his success-ful campaign for governor, Warner and I shared another private moment. He was speaking to the Virginia Education Association convened for a conference at Longwood University. I attended solely to tell him there was something I wanted to talk to him about, and he promised to stop by my office before leaving Farmville.

We were alone in the building. It was well after 5 p.m. and my co-workers had all gone home. Warner had no handlers or minders. That impressed me. It was man-to-man, nobody to keep him on message and on time. Here was a candidate for the highest office in the commonwealth sitting in an uncomfortable, decades-old chair with the editor of a small-town twice-weekly newspaper. But, as I would remind the community from time to time on the editorial pages, small-town doesn't mean small-time.

When—not if—you are elected governor, I said, would you be willing to promote Virginia's Uninsured Medical Catastrophe Fund? He wasn't familiar with the fund. I wasn't surprised. Hardly anyone in the state had heard of the UMCF, which had been conceived by me and a friend, Sarah Terry, and created by the General Assembly in 1999.

Terry and my wife, Kim, had been diagnosed with breast cancer dur-ing the same week in December 1998. During a lunch in February 1999, Terry told me about meeting a Virginia woman who'd been diagnosed with breast cancer more than a year earlier and left untreated because she was uninsured. We were both outraged, and the idea for a lifesaving fund was born in that instant. We took it to our local General Assembly representatives the next day.

Two months later, during the General Assembly's annual one-day reconvened session—commonly called "veto day"—that was held six weeks after adjournment of the regular session, the idea became law. As legislators considered gubernatorial amendments and vetoes, they approved creation of Virginia's Uninsured Medical Catastrophe Fund, even though it had not spent one second under consideration by any subcommittee or committee. The first time members of the General Assembly had a chance to consider and vote on the idea was on that final one-day session. (It had been an amendment to a piece of forestry-related legislation.)

The experience had taught me that anything could happen on "veto day." That knowledge would prove crucial later in the fight to create a state scholarship program for the casualties of massive resistance.

Meanwhile, as we talked in my small, cluttered office, I explained to Warner that this state program, administered by the Department of Medical Assistance Services, exists for one reason: to save the lives of uninsured Virginians diagnosed with a life-threatening catastrophic illness. But there is statewide ignorance of its existence. The uninsured don't know the fund can save them and nobody knows they can contribute to it through a tax check-off donation on their state income tax return, I told him. Direct corporate or individual contributions can also be made. That's all Warner needed to know. Of course, I'll do whatever I can, he agreed.

After the election, I sent Warner a congratulatory message and reminded him of his commitment. He remembered. As the newly sworn governor came out to raucous cheers at his inaugural ball in Richmond on January 12, 2002, he caught my eye across the crowd—my wife and I were in attendance—and held eye contact. Amidst everything else going on around him, he mouthed: "I haven't forgotten about you."

He meant what he'd said. Warner invited Terry and me to a press conference during the first week of April. Amid questions from the assembled media on other topics, Warner pointedly referred them to the fund and the three of us spoke about our concern for the uninsured and the UMCF's mission.

"IT'S A WONDERFUL SURPRISE," my legislative patron in the House of Delegates, Viola Baskerville, responded on April 3, 2003, when I told her I'd spoken with the governor about the scholarship proposal the previous day. "I think it's great."

That was when she mentioned contacting VCU professor Edward H. Peeples, who she thought could best document the number of individuals affected by massive resistance and therefore the potential size of the scholarship applicant pool. I mentioned in the previous chapter the numbers Peeples determined. We knew that would be important.

"In this election year," Baskerville said, "the GOP won't be able to oppose it." I shared her optimism. Election year or not, I couldn't imagine the majority of Republicans opposing it.

A few days later, Baskerville told me that Brenda Edwards, senior analyst with the Division of Legislative Services, believed draft legislation would be ready within thirty days. At Edwards's request, I faxed her my latest editorial on the Prince Edward County Scholars Fund so that she could begin the first drafting of the bill.

Baskerville also said she would contact the governor's scheduler to arrange a one-hour meeting in early May so we could follow up my phone conversation with a face-to-face meeting. Our date with the governor was set for May 8, 3–5 p.m. Two hours would provide ample opportunity to discuss the proposal at length and, I prayed, come away with the governor's full endorsement and commitment to lead the charge.

I WAS GLAD TO hear from Independent Delegate Watkins M. Abbitt Jr., a fellow Appomattox County resident who represented a portion of Prince Edward County in the House of Delegates. Abbitt's father had served in Congress and had supported the Byrd Machine and massive resistance. The younger Abbitt represented the possibilities each generation possesses to turn historical tides toward healing. No son is responsible for his father's actions. Nor are they bound to follow them if they have the courage to chart their own course.

GOP Delegate Clarke Hogan also liked the idea. Hogan had the ear of House Speaker William J. Howell and represented the largest portion of Prince Edward County. Hogan warned that my House sponsor, Delegate Baskerville, "is highly partisan," but he assured me that he was a Republican "who tries to work with her."

Hogan's observation about Baskerville concerned me. Remembering I'd selected her only because she'd helped lead the General Assembly's resolution of "profound regret" for the school closings in Prince Edward, I felt a moment's panic. Had my ignorance of any partisan baggage, from the GOP's point of view, jeopardized the scholarships' safe passage? I told myself I must dismiss such negative thoughts. But I filed Hogan's information away.

LOOKING FOR EVERY ANGLE, I called Donald P. Baker, who had retired from the *Washington Post* and was teaching at Virginia Commonwealth University in Richmond. The governor was going to be a guest in his class that very night, he told me. Not for the first or last instance, the timing was perfect. Baker said he would raise the Prince Edward Scholars Fund with Warner.

The next day, Baker briefed me on his impression of Warner's position on the scholarships. "What I read from him," Baker told me, "he thinks the proposal needs to be scaled back . . . that it's on too grand a scale." Baker said Warner questioned including grandchildren, and wondered, "When is this going to stop?"

The governor also correctly pointed out that Prince Edward was not the only locality where schools were closed and he wanted a budgetary estimate, also quite logical. But Baker said he sensed "that the governor will look for a way to make something happen."

Overall, the knowledgeable former reporter told me, he found the governor "sympathetic to the idea" but he expects Warner will look for a way to "rein this in . . . so it's not an open-ended money thing."

Baker's reconnaissance was helpful and encouraging. I shared some thoughts in response. If including the children and grandchildren of those locked out of school by massive resistance would doom the legislation, I told him, then that is an adjustment we'd have to make, whether we wanted to or not.

Virginia's massive resistance also had an impact—though much smaller and for a far shorter period of time—in Charlottesville, Front Royal, and Norfolk. But nobody could argue against the moral justice owed the five years' worth of casualties in Prince Edward, I said.

The conversation with Baker confirmed my own perception of the governor's position. He was ready to help but encouragement might be necessary, given the economic crisis dominating his, and every legislator's, radar.

THE DAY BEFORE OUR meeting with the governor, Edwards faxed me a draft of the legislation. Holding those words in my hands was like waking up and seeing your dream in bed beside you and hearing it say, "Oh, I was just dreaming about *you*." The responsibility I felt for those words, and for all the people who needed the dream to come true, brought me down to Earth. But that is where I needed to be anyway. Nobody gets to the Promised Land walking on air. Soles must be touching pavement, hallways, and, on May 8, the carpet in the third-floor conference room of the governor's office.

Warner sat at one end of the long table that nearly filled the room. I was to his immediate left. Several members of his administration were present. Among those joining Delegate Baskerville and me to discuss the scholarship legislation were John Stokes, Edward H. Peeples, Brenda Edwards, Vonita Foster—a leader of the Lest We Forget Foundation that raised scholarship funds for college-bound children of those locked out of Prince Edward County's schools—and Delegate Abbitt.

As he had during our April 2 phone conversation and in his April 28 comments relayed to me by Baker, Warner focused heavily on the money issue. "The state is broke," he declared, adding for emphasis, "Chapter 11."

Warner also equated the five years of school closings in Prince Edward with other wounding manifestations of Jim Crow. If the state creates these scholarships, he said, others would come forward claiming something needed to be done in response to their own suffering.

No, I emphatically told him, thinking of John Hurt, there is "no parallel" in Virginia to the wounds from massive resistance in Prince Edward, for which the state had expressed its "profound regret" just a few months earlier. I made that point as forcefully as I could without being disrespectful.

The governor also expressed concern that Virginia would be embarrassed nationally if, on the fiftieth anniversary of the *Brown* decision, the General Assembly defeated creation of scholarships for the casualties of massive resistance to that landmark decision. I completely understood Warner's concern. But surrendering to fear in the spring of 2003 would bring its own kind of shame.

As the meeting was coming to a close, the governor turned, looked me in the eye and finally declared his position with clear intent. "I'll fight with you on this," he said.

There would be no capitulation. That was the Mark Warner I knew. Those were the only words I needed to hear. Words I would never forget.

The governor added that he would get a legal review of the constitutionality of using lottery funds for the scholarships. I was glad to hear he was already thinking about the next step—funding. Without the money, "scholarship" was just a word waiting for its definition to be fulfilled.

I left the meeting exuberant, believing that we had secured the most important of all political allies in the commonwealth. After that initial joy, however, I could not help but remind myself that the governor's declaration had come at the end of a meeting during which he spent much of the time expressing his doubts. This began to gnaw at me. Warner clearly said he would fight with us. But his unspoken opinion seemed to be that the scholarships had as much chance of winning passage in the General Assembly as a snowflake surviving the Fourth of July.

It was characteristic of the extraordinary upside-down and inside-out *Brown* Scholarship crusade that, in the end, both Warner's 20–20 concerns and my blind faith would be completely justified.

I DID NOT DOUBT that Warner meant it when he turned to me and said "I'll fight with you on this." But I was convinced that he would feel far more confident if he had reinforcements. During the two-hour drive home to Appomattox, I began to strategize how to get former governors Linwood Holton, Charles Robb, Gerald Baliles, and Doug Wilder to stand with him. (Holton, a Republican, served 1970–74; Robb, 1982–86; Baliles, 1986–90; and Wilder, 1990–94. The latter three were Democrats.)

My determination to enlist that foursome was strengthened on May 13 after Democratic House of Delegates member Ken Plum said he should have warned me that he regarded Warner as too cautious by nature, probably as a result of his business background.

If the self-made millionaire was overly cautious, he came by it honestly. Warner has made it no secret that his first two business ventures utterly failed. Losing everything and sleeping in a car or on a friend's couch will make anyone cautious. But Warner must not have been too cautious, in my opinion, given his ultimate financial success at the cutting edge of the telecommunications/cellular revolution. Risks had to be taken as Warner accumulated his life's fortune, and I was hoping the same spirit of adventure would benefit the scholarship crusade.

The strategy would give Warner the added political muscle of four ex-governors who, I believed, would embrace the chance to publicly stand in support of the scholarship legislation at the key moment next January. Those four men could make all the difference. They would draw public and political support and their announcement would attract media coverage, all of which I believed would be crucial given the understandable preoccupation at the Capitol with the state's economic crisis.

All I had to do was track them down and persuade these former governors to join the team.

Before the end of the month, I had spoken directly with Holton, Robb, and Baliles about my plan for a joint statement of support for the *Brown* Scholarships when the legislature convened in January of 2004.

The fourth? Not even by the end of the year.

Why leave out former Republican governors George Allen (1994–98) and James Gilmore (1998–2002)? I regarded both men as extremely partisan. I lobbied GOP and Democratic legislators who represented Prince Edward County, but I was afraid that alerting those two prominent Republicans about my strategy might prompt a preemptive strike by state-level GOP operatives against Warner and the scholarship legislation. Warner's great anxiety over defeat in the GOP-controlled General Assembly was no argument against keeping Allen and Gilmore out of the loop for the time being.

I had nothing personal against the two men. Allen had appointed me as a regional chairman of his statewide *Opportunity Virginia* economic development initiative. Allen told me he could think of nobody with a louder voice of advocacy for Southside Virginia. I'm a liberal, but I play well with others. Differing political points of view never prevent me from seeking creative collaboration for the greater good. I may indeed have been doing Gilmore and Allen a disservice. But I knew that I would reach out to them later, in time to join the other governors when it mattered most and when it was too late for partisan politics to sabotage the plan.

ON MAY 23, 2003, I spoke with Holton. He promised to review the information I was sending him on the scholarship proposal and consider what he could do. Holton cautioned, however, that he made sure that whatever he did was a plus for his son-in-law, then the lieutenant governor. It was no secret that Tim Kaine had ambitions to succeed Warner. After all, who willingly settles for a political career that ends with the second-highest elected office in the state?

Four days later, I reached Robb. The former governor told me he had been purposely staying below the public horizon. But he added, "for something like this I might make an exception." Robb made a point of telling me he wanted to be careful about giving me "too much hope" but that the concept was one that interested him. Robb and Holton would talk about it.

"Robb and I talked. We are certainly supportive of the concept," Holton told me a few days later, "and we suggest you send the same material to Baliles and then the three of us will talk about it and we'll get back to you."

Holton, the state's sixty-first governor, had been elected in November 1969 as Virginia's first Republican governor since Reconstruction. During his first year in office, he had reacted to court-ordered busing in Virginia by voluntarily sending his three children to predominantly black public schools in Richmond. Holton could have sent his children to school anywhere. One of them, his daughter, Anne, was by 2003 married to Lieutenant Governor Kaine.

The salt-of-the-earth gentleman from Big Stone Gap in southwest Virginia led by example. Holton wrote in his memoir, *Opportunity Time:*

I was exuberant that morning. Supported by a believing family, and confident that most Virginians and certainly posterity would agree, I proclaimed by one simple act that 'Virginia is part of this Republic, and Virginia will comply with its laws.' In other words, we were putting our actions and our children where my mouth was. This commitment of Virginia's first family implemented, through very visible *deeds*, the *words* of my inaugural address: "The era of defiance is behind us," and "Let our goal in Virginia be an aristocracy of ability, regardless of race, color or creed."

A NEARLY HALF-HOUR PHONE conversation with Baliles on June 2 poured the first footers for the foundation of a crucial relationship. He liked the idea and would certainly help.

Baliles had led an extraordinary ticket when he followed Robb into the governor's office. He was inaugurated in 1986 along with the first African American and the first woman elected to statewide office in Virginia: Lieutenant Governor L. Douglas Wilder and Attorney General Mary Sue Terry. The trio of Democrats had comprised what *Encyclopedia Virginia* describes as "the most diverse ticket Virginia had seen." By far. They became the faces of a changing Virginia.

The former governor told me on the phone from his Hunton & Williams law office in Richmond, "You've got a good case here. You can make this happen. I will provide advice and counsel as you go forward. Keep the information flow on a need-to-know basis or people will jump out of hedgerows at you."

That last warning reinforced my decision to keep Gilmore and Allen at a distance regarding the joint statement strategy until the danger of an effective ambush passed. I may have been paranoid, but Baliles's need-to-know advice supported my gut feeling.

"Continue to quietly seek support and advice," he urged.

CONTINUING TO SEEK FORMER Governor Wilder's support, however, got me nowhere. Let's put it this way: They say the best way to eat an elephant is one bite at a time. Reaching my fourth governor felt like trying to eat a herd of stampeding elephants with a plastic fork and a rubber knife.

It would take eight months—deep inside the dark winter days of 2004—before I finally communicated directly with Wilder. The delay wasn't for lack of trying or because I did not have contact information for him. I had an office address and phone number. I would have several phone numbers and a fax number by the end. It was just that Doug Wilder is, well, Doug Wilder.

A maverick is a horse, or a person, who wears no man's brand. I regard Doug Wilder as such a maverick that he often refuses to wear his *own* brand.

And he savors it.

The grandson of former slaves, Wilder's independence is seared deep within the Korean War Bronze Star recipient. His distinct brand of individuality served him well during a historic political journey in a former Confederate state. Becoming the first African American elected to statewide office in Virginia, and then the first black governor in the U.S., would require creatively determined runs through racist stereotypes—not to mention partisan political scheming—that would attempt to fell him.

Encyclopedia Virginia notes that Wilder had "volunteered for combat duty to reduce his service time. At Pork Chop Hill, he and two other men found themselves cut off from their unit, but they bluffed nineteen Chinese soldiers into surrendering."

Wilder was undaunted by the political landscape in Virginia.

He had graduated from Virginia Union University in 1951, shortly after the Prince Edward County students went on strike at Robert R. Moton High School. He earned his law degree from Howard University and set up private practice in Richmond during the summer of 1959. The state had only recently pulled back from its massive resistance to *Brown,* but Prince Edward County was right in the midst of shutting down its public school system, and the Commonwealth didn't seem to mind at all. State tuition grants would help whites to afford the whites-only Prince Edward Academy.

Who wouldn't want to be a maverick in a state like that? Wilder had gone on to corral and brand history with his own name.

GOVERNOR WARNER HAD NOTHING to do with crafting and packaging the reparation legislation and the intensity of his commitment to the scholarships remained a nagging question. Would he remain in the trenches or go over the top with us? The focus and energy needed to resolve the state's fiscal crisis might swamp and sap him. But, I thought, don't tell me "I'll fight with you on this" and then not show up.

Delegate Hogan told me on May 28 that he'd met with the governor the previous day. During that meeting, which focused on other issues, Hogan said he had brought up the scholarships. "I think he's amenable," the Republican delegate told me. "The question is how to put forward the funding . . . I think we've got an ally, but I don't think he's going to kill himself on it."

Warner is a remarkable man. His rebound from two failed business ventures into financial and political ascendancy speaks of deep personal inner resources that money cannot buy. Getting up from life's canvas once is admirable. Doing so twice demonstrated the qualities I hoped he'd bring to the *Brown* Scholarship crusade. I wasn't asking him to kill himself, but a determined commitment meant doing whatever was necessary, short of providing work for an undertaker.

MEANWHILE, DONALD P. BAKER made certain I had the details of the other massive resistance school closings in Virginia. Baliles had told me it was important to get "precise information" on that piece of Virginia's history. All of those were white schools, Baker explained in an email, because whites weren't trying to integrate black schools, and so the black schools remained open. Six Norfolk schools were closed—three high schools and three junior high schools. A high school and an elementary school in Charlottesville and a high school in Warren County were closed.

In each instance, Baker noted, the schools closed in September 1958. The Norfolk and Charlottesville schools reopened on February 2, 1959, with Warren County High School in Front Royal reopening on February 18 after Virginia abandoned its formal policy of massive resistance to the *Brown* decision.

Those closings certainly had a negative impact, but nothing like the life-changing fallout in Prince Edward County where the entire county public school system was shut down for sixty months. To put that length of time into perspective, when schools were closed in Prince Edward County, Elvis was king and most Americans had never heard of Liverpool,

England. When the schools reopened, the Beatles ruled the music world.

More seriously, when the Prince Edward County Board of Supervisors went to war against public education in 1959, most Americans didn't know North or South Vietnam existed. By 1964 . . .

The small group of us who had met with Warner in May worked with the Division of Legislative Services, and before the end of the summer the legislation we hoped would make the scholarship reparation real was written and ready to be filed for the 2004 session of the General Assembly.

We were taking a two-pronged approach: one bill of language to create the program and a separate budget amendment to provide the funds.

The name was also changed from the Prince Edward County Scholars Fund to the *Brown v. Board of Education* Scholarship Program and Fund. The color-blind scholarships would be available, as they legally and morally must, to any Virginia resident, black or white, affected by massive resistance in Charlottesville, Norfolk, and Warren County, as well as in Prince Edward County. Naming it for Prince Edward County—even though Prince Edward was ground zero for massive resistance—was inviting legislators to dismiss it as too narrowly focused on one community.

Furthermore, the fiftieth anniversary of the *Brown* decision would be celebrated in the spring of 2004. That could only help our cause.

Unfortunately, the legislation could not include the children and grandchildren of those locked out of school by massive resistance. The state's constitution, we were told, would not allow it. We couldn't prove damages to the children. Though children might be affected because their mother was struck by a car, I was told by way of an example, they are not legally due damages because they were not directly impacted: they weren't struck by the car.

Baliles responded favorably to the bill-crafting. He liked the two-prong approach—one bill to create the program and the budget amendment to make the scholarships be, well, scholarships. Changing the name to the *Brown v. Board of Education* Scholarship Program and Fund, along with the bifurcated approach, he added, "may serve you well."

Not everyone agreed.

One bill to create the program and a separate budget amendment is, Delegate Hogan admitted when I briefed him, a "tactical question." But, he didn't want that "bifurcated approach to give the General Assembly an out" not to fund the scholarship program after creating it.

Scholarships devoid of money?

A Trojan Horse with nothing inside it couldn't possibly be rolled out in Prince Edward County, could it?

As summer was ending I received a note from Robb, words I would not throw away:

"You are engaged in a noble effort," wrote the man elected governor in 1981, preceding Baliles, and who served in the U.S. Senate from 1989 to 2001. "And if Linwood Holton and Jerry Baliles are agreeable as well we'll indicate our support collectively at the appropriate time."

The Phoenix, Arizona, native was raised just outside the nation's capital in Alexandria, Virginia. *Encyclopedia Virginia* states that after graduating from college, Robb had "joined the U.S. Marine Corps, graduating with honors from the Marine training school in Quantico, Virginia. That led to an assignment as a social aide at the White House, where he met and later married Lynda Bird Johnson." Her father was President Lyndon B. Johnson, who did so much to ensure passage of the Civil Rights Act of 1964.

Robb's character as a young man is demonstrated by the fact that he left the comforts of Washington, D.C., and served two tours of combat duty in Vietnam where, states *Encyclopedia Virginia*, "he commanded a rifle company and won a Bronze Star."

Robb thanked me for keeping him posted and explained that he had been out of the country for two weeks "or I'd have gotten back [to you] sooner."

I put a copy of his note in my Bible.

Joan Johns Cobbs had been in the auditorium on that historic 1951 day when her older sister began to address the student body at Robert R. Moton High School.

"When she got up on the stage at the assembly and started to speak, I was so shocked at what she was saying that I squirmed down in my seat," Cobbs had told me for a story in the *Farmville Herald* about finding her sister's handwritten recollections.

"I was afraid and shocked and everything and couldn't imagine her doing this . . . And Barbara was only sixteen. It's mind-boggling when you think about it now. But she was not the type to be afraid. I don't understand it," said Cobbs, "but whatever she felt like she should do in terms of anything, she just didn't seem to be afraid."

John Stokes had asked me to call Joan and tell her about the *Brown* Scholarship legislation. Speaking to me in 2003 from her New Jersey home, Cobbs said, "We've been hurt so long. No one seemed to care. No one seemed to give any thought to doing anything like this. I'm very happy you're doing this."

When I hung up the telephone, I felt the words of the prophet Jeremiah reverberating through me. That the balm for Gilead might be appearing through the editor of the once-segregationist *Farmville Herald* could only deepen the healing. What historical irony: the story coming full circle in a way nobody could have imagined.

Nor was I alone. One voice may cry out in the wilderness but only people, joined in common purpose, can transform it. It was our turn to try. The 2004 session of the General Assembly was upon us.

6

Into the Sausage Grinder

During one of the many conversations I had with former governor Gerald Baliles, he reminded me of the old saying that people shouldn't watch sausage being made or legislation becoming law. I would learn he was not guilty of overstatement.

As the *Brown* Scholarship dream disappeared into the machinations of the 2004 session of the General Assembly there were times when I thought it would be ground up, its remains scattered grotesquely across the abattoir floor in the House and Senate.

The legislative process was over almost as quickly as it began, barely getting out of the Higher Education Subcommittee of the House Education Committee on January 22. The subcommittee chairman tried to kill the bill by recommending that HB 846 be carried over to the next session. "Carried over" is the equivalent of being taken to the undertaker with orders to bury immediately. Exhumation in twelve months during the 2005 legislative session would merely be a possibility.

My fears escalated when another subcommittee member expressed concern about giving any false hope by passing the bill without an assurance of funding.

Another delegate wondered why we weren't going to the Prince Edward County Board of Supervisors to fund the scholarships, a question that, while germane, displayed no understanding of the state's role in massive resistance, nor recognition of the profound regret expressed by the General Assembly just the previous year. Nor did it take into account the use for a time of state-funded tuition grants by students at the private, all-white Prince Edward Academy.

Fortunately, Republican delegate Steve Landes and two other subcommittee members spoke for the bill, acknowledging that the state shared responsibility for the school closings. Landes offered an amendment—a four-year sunset clause—that meant if the scholarship program wasn't doing what it was established to do, it would be revisited by legislators four years down the road.

Neither Delegate Baskerville nor I had any difficulty with walking down that road. There was no doubt in my mind that it would be well traveled by scholarship applicants and recipients throughout those four years.

On a voice vote, as I reported in the *Farmville Herald*, there wasn't a single "nay."

The relief was enormous.

We also knew the funding target.

The budget amendment for the scholarships—the second part of the bifurcated approach—totaled $2 million. Though this was much less than I'd advocated—based on that $369,000 in state funds for the 1958 Prince Edward County school year in today's dollar value—it did essentially amount to five years of $369,000.*

During the subcommittee meeting, however, Watkins Abbitt, an Independent legislator who'd dropped his Democratic Party affiliation to take the GOP's bull's-eye off his back, stunned us by telling subcommittee members that we did not expect any state funding.

Furthermore, in the hallway after the subcommittee meeting, Abbitt asked Baskerville to "withdraw" the budget amendment.

Baskerville and I were firm. "No way" was that budget amendment going to be withdrawn, and I told Abbitt that former governors were waiting for the right moment—very soon—to issue a joint statement of support.

To suggest withdrawing the budget amendment after we'd cleared the

---

* With inflation, the state's $369,000 appropriation in 1958 would have been roughly the equivalent of $2.35 million in 2003–2004 dollars, or approximately $11.75 million over five years, which is the calculation upon which I'd based my original funding argument for the *Brown* Scholarships.

subcommittee hurdle seemed the very definition of defeatist. Abbitt undoubtedly thought he was advancing a pragmatic way to create the scholarships. In fact, his declaration to subcommittee members might have helped to win their vote to forward the legislation to the full education committee.

But—and this would become the march-to-battle mantra—scholarships without funding are not scholarships.

Abbitt, with his years of political experience, must have known that, yes, it *was* possible for the scholarship program to pass without funding. Delegate Hogan had warned me about that, too. But I was absolutely certain we would not condone taking the money away ourselves.

THE NEXT STEP IN the House of Delegates was before the Education Committee, and it was politically and meteorologically slippery. A fierce snowstorm was forecast and a predawn drive to Richmond by Rita Moseley and me would likely be impossible. I feared that our critical testimony to the committee would be stranded in the drifting snow.

When the schools were closed and locked in 1959, Moseley was twelve years old. She was out of school entirely the first two years and then, in 1961, her mother drove her to Blacksburg, Virginia, three hours away. Moseley had never been there before. Nor had she ever met the family with whom she would live for the next two years of her young life while attending schools there. Moseley would not see Farmville and her family again until the summer of 1963.

She was not alone in becoming a stranger in a strange land. Good people across the state and the nation accepted children from Prince Edward County into their homes to help the youngsters fill the educational abyss in their lives. However, those amounted to a small percentage of the 2,200-plus black children left on the wrong side of the "no trespassing" signs.

"I always thought about how my mother sacrificed me going back to school, sending her only daughter to live with strangers," Moseley would tell me for a 2013 story in the *Farmville Herald*. "I feel compassion, how she sacrificed her feelings, and everything, just to make sure I got my education."

I wanted the committee members to hear the voice and look into the eyes of someone who had lived the result of massive resistance. Moseley did graduate from high school, but those five years had left scars.

Scrambling, I threw a few necessities into a small suitcase and drove east from Appomattox, away from the approaching storm, to pick up Moseley in Farmville on Sunday afternoon. I explained that we would stay at a hotel within walking distance of the General Assembly. Her response was, "Let's go." We had to.

General Assembly committee meetings are held regardless of weather conditions and whether the public, including those asked to testify, can get there. So much work had been done since February 18, 2003, to reach this moment. We'd come too far to give the appearance to committee members that supporters of the *Brown* Scholarship legislation would not brave a snowstorm for their cause.

We barely beat the snow to Richmond. That night Moseley and I sat down in the hotel restaurant next to its huge windows. The view made us feel as if we were in one of those snow-globes that children shake to create a magical world unto itself, a world of happily ever after, not unlike the one of Barbara Rose Johns's dreams.

Here was the editor of the newspaper that had fought so hard to lock Moseley and her classmates out of school having dinner with her the night before both of them would testify on behalf of the editor's plan to give back the educational opportunity those closed schools had stolen.

The next morning, Moseley and I slogged carefully through the snow toward the House Education Committee meeting. After a nearly sleepless night, I had gotten my speech for the committee right where I wanted it. But I never said a word. The committee wasn't keen on hearing what we had to say. They were prepared to move the bill forward, but only after deleting the reference to an appropriation. The deletion wouldn't matter, it was noted, because the budget amendment would override the committee's amendment: If, that is, the budget amendment passed the House.

Because it seemed clear that the committee would appreciate hearing from only one of us, I urged Moseley to speak. It was important to me that whatever happened next, at least one of the casualties of massive resistance would have had the chance to look the Commonwealth of Virginia in the eye and speak about what had been done and what the scholarships could do about it so many years later.

Moseley spoke directly and honestly to the committee members about her experience of massive resistance and what the scholarship program would mean to her and others who had been locked out of school. The full text of her remarks is included as part of her book, *No School.*

"I often wonder what I could have done, what I could have been, if my education had not been interrupted. The horrible act that was done to us as little children when they closed our schools for five years damaged and changed our lives in many ways," she told them. "I see it firsthand on a daily basis. Some of us would have been in first grade and some of us would have graduated from high school the year our schools were closed. Some of us were out of school for the entire time. Some of us did not go back to school at all. Some of us are still hurt, angry and still cry with tears running down their faces. Grown men and women . . . The passing of this bill is very important. There is no question in my mind of the good the passing of this bill would do. . . ."

The committee's decision to cut the word "appropriation" was more frigid to me than the weather. Afterward, I heard Abbitt repeat the advice given us after the House subcommittee meeting last week. Withdraw the budget amendment, he told Baskerville.

I shook my head. Nothing says "move forward" quite like "withdraw."

Baskerville, of course, did nothing of the kind. She and I shared the apparently bizarre opinion that scholarships are, in fact, a monetary grant allowing the recipients to pursue their education.

I was glad that Moseley's voice had spoken for those wounded by massive resistance. I was deeply thankful that she knew it had been heard. She kept telling me I should have been the one to speak. No way, I replied, it had to be you.

In one sense, it had been a successful committee vote. The legislation to establish the *Brown* Scholarship program had survived the House Education Committee. That gave us something to hang onto and fight for. But I was feeling distinctly blue driving back to Farmville. Removal of any reference to an appropriation, and Abbitt's continued insistence that the budget amendment be withdrawn, were opening my eyes and I did not like what I was seeing. I was afraid Abbitt had his finger on the pulse of the House. And, given the way Baskerville was viewed by many House Republicans, Abbitt's presence as a political wingman at both the sub-committee and committee meetings was probably more important than I knew.

ON JANUARY 30, AMENDED House Bill 846 passed the full House of Delegates. The majority accepted the House Education Committee's recommendation. The word "appropriations" was deleted.

Deletion of "appropriations" would have encouraged only those who believed the scholarships should be privately funded. A state scholarship program with no state funding would be no act of reparation or healing. How profound was the 2003 House resolution of "profound regret" over the state's role in massive resistance? At that point, I was just asking.

The amended HB 846 was sent to the Senate, where it was referred to the Senate's Education Committee.

Then the legislative path twisted again. The Senate Finance Committee had approved SB 230 with an amendment *requiring* state funds be appropriated this budget cycle or the scholarship program created by the bill would not exist. This was the complete opposite of HB 846 that had entirely removed the word "appropriations."

The Senate Finance Committee declared:

> That the provisions of this act (SB 230) shall not become effective unless an appropriation of general funds effectuating the purposes of this act is included in the general appropriation act for the period of July 1, 2004 through June 30, 2006, passed during the 2004 session of the General Assembly.

If the Senate Finance Committee meant to make certain that state funds were in the budget, the amendment would be a lifesaver, *if* the House agreed to the Senate proviso. But, if the House stuck to its no-appropriation guns, the Senate requirement would doom the *Brown* Scholarship legislation.

It all seemed dependent on the conference committee, in which a small number of delegates and senators reconcile the differences in specific bills and the budget proposals from their respective chambers.

But I'd had a backup strategy in mind for months. No matter what the General Assembly did during the regular session, I knew that Governor Warner *could* send down his own budget amendment for consideration during the one-day reconvened or veto session that would be held six weeks after the regular session ended. On that day, anything was possible as legislators considered the governor's vetoes and last-minute amendments. As mentioned earlier, Sarah Terry and I had learned that political truth when Virginia's Uninsured Medical Catastrophe Fund was created during the reconvened session in 1999.

That was another reason it was so important for Warner to fight beside us and publicly support state funding—in the best-case scenario, the existing $2 million budget amendments. Even if the General Assembly defeated them, however—and the House had seemed adamantly opposed so far—the governor would be positioned to act on his own during the veto session. General Assembly passage would still be needed on that day, but the political dynamic, I felt certain, would be totally changed in our favor. By then, I hoped, the media from around the state and across the nation would be watching. There would be far less political cover and far more political accountability on that one day of voting by legislators.

When I told the governor's press secretary, Ellen Qualls, about the Senate Finance Committee amendment, she called it a worst-case scenario. No, I replied, it was an opportunity to take the amendment as a Senate endorsement that words are not enough, that "scholarships" are nothing without funding. We could use the amendment as a springboard to higher moral ground.

That *is* one way of looking at it, she said, in a way that felt like she was patting my head and hoping I'd get over whatever it was that had given me a fever.

The bottom line, I stressed in a later voice mail to Qualls, was getting the legislation to the governor's desk.

THE END OF THE legislative session was rapidly approaching, but funding for the scholarships was nowhere to be found in the GOP-controlled House, and there wasn't much time to do anything about it.

The 2004 General Assembly had convened on January 14 for a sixty-day session that was scheduled to end on March 16. We were now more than halfway to that finish line. At this point, the House of Delegates' GOP majority was determined that not a penny of the $2 million budget amendment to make the *Brown* Scholarships real would survive. Everything depended upon the budget amendment winning passage in the Senate. That would send the funding question to the House and Senate conference committee to negotiate between the zero funding coming from the House and, I hoped, $2 million from the Senate.

On Sunday, February 22, the House and Senate money committees were scheduled to make public their respective versions of the proposed state budget. Senator Lambert's position on the Senate Finance Committee could prove crucial. What kind of political strings might he pull to secure a place for the full $2 million in the Senate's budget?

It soon became clear that Lambert faced a difficult challenge. Senate passage of SB 230 created the *Brown v. Board of Education* Scholarship Program, as the House had done with HB 846. But Prince Edward County's state senator, Republican Frank Ruff estimated funding had a "50–50" chance of getting through the legislature's upper chamber.

THE SCHEDULE FOR UNVEILING the final Senate and House budgets began to twist and turn as well, reflecting the entrenchment on both sides of the state budget battle. Few Republican delegates were willing to join their Senate GOP colleagues in pursuing additional revenue to solve the economic issues facing the state. The vote would be close and the proposed 2004–2006 biennium budgets coming from each chamber would not be identical. This would mean some kind of compromise and yet another vote by the House and the Senate on a final conference committee budget proposal.

I had hopes for the Senate until Lambert called me on February 23.

He said there was $100,000 in the Senate budget for the *Brown v. Board of Education* Scholarship Program and Fund. Initially, there had been nothing, just as in the House, but Lambert said he had gone to finance committee chairman Senator John Chichester and persuaded him to support $50,000 for each year of the biennium.

The amount could be "adjusted" for the 2004–2006 budget's second year, the senator assured me. So at least, Lambert explained, if anyone applies for a scholarship there will be funding, and if we need more money we could try next year.

The senator said he believed the $100,000 appropriation would get through both the full Senate and the conference committee and thus into the new state budget.

I was incredulous. My Senate patron was enthused over $100,000 rather than the $2 million budget amendment to support his own legislation.

"We don't want to put a million [a year] in," he told me. "[Massive resistance] was fifty years ago; we don't know how many people" will apply for scholarships. But, he continued, it would also be "embarrassing if there was no money."

I was embarrassed by the $100,000.

"If we need more money, I think we can get it [next year]," the senator repeated.

Yes, this was *something*, and $100,000 more than the House of Delegates had approved so far. Yet the meager sum punched me in the gut more forcefully than no money at all. My reaction may have been irrational, but the $100,000 seemed to place a value upon the scholarships and the suffering caused by massive resistance. I found that valuation outrageous.

Disgusted, I immediately called Baskerville and left a voice mail message that I thought the Senate's $100,000 was "pathetic."

A $2 million "veto day" budget amendment from Governor Warner now seemed the only path to full funding. Needing to educate myself on the finer points of that process, I reached out to Frank B. Atkinson, an attorney with Hunton & Williams who had served as a senior U.S. Justice Department official in the Reagan administration. More to the point of my call, however, this prominent Republican had been legal counsel to Governor Allen.

I knew Atkinson because we'd served together on the board of directors of Hampden-Sydney College's Wilson Center for Leadership in the Public Interest. By the time we hung up, I was glad I'd called him. He would, I felt, become a valuable ally down the road and his insight and guidance were immediately beneficial.

Atkinson confirmed that after Warner received the state budget, following the conference committee's action, the governor could then propose an amendment for the veto session. I knew that, but I wanted to learn the logistics, nuances, and any legislative code words that might be helpful. The request for that budget amendment, I felt certain, would come from me.

Warner could do nothing now, Atkinson advised, because the budget was "not before him." Virginia, Atkinson added, is one of the few states that allow a governor to delve back into the budget in such a fashion—but not until the General Assembly reconvenes sixty days after the regular session ends.

The *Brown* Scholarships, he emphatically told me, are "a great cause." Because his voice resonated with such respect and depth in key GOP circles, I knew the day would come when I would ask him to speak to Republicans on behalf of full funding. His enthusiasm for the scholarships would be a valuable political tool.

A vote during the veto session, Atkinson continued, confirming my view of the altered political dynamic and resulting pro-scholarship leverage of that moment, "would create public accountability."

Precisely. That was the path veto day could open through the General Assembly's budget barriers.

No more under-the-radar zero funding. Everybody would be watching.

"There is cover now" for General Assembly members, Atkinson said. A veto day showdown "would force them out."

The time had come to begin what might become a lengthy veto day budget amendment pitch to Warner. I wanted him to commit to a budget amendment. To ensure accountability and follow-through, I wanted him to do so publicly.

AFTER LYING AWAKE ALL night in turmoil over what Senator Lambert had told me, I awoke determined to convince him to fight for full funding. On February 24, I faxed a letter to his office:

> After thinking about what you told me yesterday about not asking

for $1 million this year because the school closings were fifty years ago, I must respectfully disagree. I believe we should press the conferees to fund SB 230 and HB 846 for the original $2 million budget amendment. With a four-year sunset clause, if there is no demand for the scholarships, then the money reverts to the state and $2 million is a tiny fraction of a $59 billion budget.

We know there were 2,500 students who lost their educational opportunity in Prince Edward, 2,200-plus black and about 250 white. We estimate that 10 percent is a realistic conservative estimate, or 250 who would take advantage of this opportunity; $50,000 next year would be $200 each and that does nothing.

I'm afraid too many people would view $50,000 as going from massive resistance to Dismissive Assistance that wouldn't pay for the letter J in justice.

The $2 million equals what the state would have spent on the education of these very same people between 1959–1964. In 1958 the state spent $369,000 in Prince Edward. Multiplied by five years of closed schools that is $1.8-plus million in yesterday's dollars and no interest. The money was meant for these people and their education. It's been sitting in Richmond for decades. Appropriate it now. This is not new funding or a new program. Also, these families continued to pay state taxes that were used to fund public education for every other locality in the state even as theirs was taken from them for five years,"

I wrote, trying to answer every argument. I simply could not understand anyone truly believing the $2 million was unjustified . . .

We need to fight, Senator Lambert, and you need to lead that fight, sir.

I accept that I could have, probably should have, done more before this to make Lambert and me closer teammates, as I had with Delegate Baskerville. But I was doing so now.

As backup, however, I began a series of calls to the office of Senator Henry Marsh, speaking to his legislative aide, asking for the spread of "gas and matches." We needed to light a fire under Lambert and the rest of the Senate, and I was hoping to get the Black Legislative Caucus involved.

To increase the pressure and leverage, I wanted to bring the *Washington Post* into the funding fight, so I left a message with its Richmond bureau. I also called Oliver Hill, and the legendary civil rights attorney said, yes, he would encourage Marsh and Lambert to fight for the funding. Marsh had clerked for Hill out of law school and became a partner in Hill's Richmond law firm. My instincts were telling me the time had come to enlist someone else to lead the Senate charge, no matter who the legislation's patron was, and Marsh would be the man I'd ask first.

In a February 25 fax, I told him

> I implore you with all the fervor I can muster to lead the General Assembly, as Virginia stands at this historic crossroads, to fully fund the $2 million budget amendment in the biennium budget for the *Brown v. Board of Education* Scholarship Program and Fund, HB 846 and SB 230, which have passed the General Assembly without a dissenting vote but need the funding to make them real and anything but a mockery . . . Please, Senator Marsh, before it is too late.

The fight needed to be taken to the floor of the Senate. This was no time to settle for a separate and unequal funding seat at the back of the budget bus, shoved out the emergency exit and clinging to the back bumper. And, in the House of Delegates, not even allowed on the bus.

7

Destroy the Headline to Save It?

Moments after I sent the fax to Marsh, Jo Becker of the *Washington Post* called, changing everything. But there would have been no media calls without the February 13 joint statement of Governors Warner, Holton, Robb, and Baliles supporting the *Brown* Scholarships and funding to make them real.

While the political machinations in the General Assembly were under-way, I had been fighting another desperate battle behind the scenes. Week after week, the time for Warner and the former governors to make their public stand was passing us by. The strategy I had begun working on in May 2003 proved far more important—and much harder to pull off—than I ever imagined. It would eventually feel like "the joint statement from hell."

When Baliles and I spoke on January 12, he advised me to give all of the former governors the complete picture—send them a copy of the legislation, a request to join in a statement of support, and press clippings. I followed my counselor's advice, wondering how much gubernatorial company Warner would have by his side as he stood with us.

And what of Warner himself? He and his administration had been silent since our "I'll fight with you on this" meeting seven months earlier. No press releases had been issued and no mention was made in his early January "state of the commonwealth" address. Warner's ambitious legislative proposal to provide a comprehensive solution to the budget crisis took center stage, as it should have. But I was disappointed he hadn't at least mentioned the scholarship initiative. With the eyes and ears of the General Assembly and the media paying close attention, along with a listening statewide audience, the speech would have been an effective and fitting place to begin fighting by our side.

But four days later I saw the governor at the Robert Russa Moton Museum in Farmville, and he raised the issue of the *Brown* Scholarships himself. It was on his radar after all. "Thank you," he told me on January 16, "for holding our feet to the fire on all of this."

I smiled and replied, "Thank you for having your feet held to the fire."

He looked me straight in the eye and said, "No, you're a good man."

That brief exchange eased my concern about Warner's commitment

As yet, Warner knew nothing of my plan to rally former governors in support of the scholarships and, in effect, his own advocacy of the legislation. The time had obviously come to tell Warner. Tell him confidentially, Baliles advised, to give Warner the chance to lead the charge: "He might want to come out for it first and not be usurped or have the appearance of coming in last." Baliles said to assure Warner that the former governors "are willing to step in publicly after him or go first, if he prefers. But give him the opportunity to publicly endorse it first."

I UNVEILED THE JOINT statement plan to the governor through press secretary Ellen Qualls. She sounded excited about the added support, saying she would talk to Warner the following morning. The next day I'd have the chance to personally tell Warner about the joint statement strategy.

In Richmond for the first House of Delegates' subcommittee meeting on January 22, I stopped by the governor's office first. Qualls told me she hadn't been able to brief the governor yet on the joint statement. Instead, Warner at that moment came out of his private office, and she told him to speak with me there and then. Perfect timing.

Our conversation occurred as we walked downstairs from the third floor of the Capitol; the governor was on his way to the Executive Mansion. I told Warner about the plans for a joint statement from as many former governors as possible, joining him in a public endorsement of the *Brown v. Board of Education* Scholarship Program and Fund.

The governor told me he was "with the legislation heart and soul" but he wanted a dollar amount. I told him I expected to get the precise funding figure that evening. Warner said, "If it's a number I can live with, then I'd love to endorse the scholarships in concert with the other governors and let it get the attention it deserves."

I replied that I'd gotten through to everyone but Governor Wilder, adding that I believed Wilder would "come on."

Warner smiled. "Ken, Ken, you and I have been around this awhile. Don't ever assume Doug Wilder will do anything."

Leaving the General Assembly building in the early winter darkness, I ran into Qualls and gave her the good subcommittee news. I also told her the budget amendment was for $2 million and asked that she pass that information to Warner.

My next step, however, was off a cliff I never saw. Neither Warner nor Baliles wanted to issue the joint statement without Wilder signed on, Qualls told me on January 26. "Keep working Wilder," she advised.

I'd been trying to reach Wilder for nearly eight months. I disagreed with their reluctance to move forward without him. A joint statement by three former governors—Holton, Robb, and Baliles—and Warner hardly seemed worthless. Delegate Baskerville's reaction to this bit of news—"to hell with Wilder; we're not going to let one man hold it hostage"—was identical to my own.

"Chickenshit," she said of Warner and Baliles's reluctance to issue the joint statement without Wilder.

At least a ton of it, I thought.

Baliles did his best to explain. If the statement is released without Wilder then Wilder "becomes the story. And you don't want to step on your own headline," he told me.

Yes, but at least there would *be* a headline.

When I asked for his help in getting through to Wilder, Baliles described himself as "the last one to ask . . . I don't have a number to reach him."

Governors began to fall like dominoes. On January 26, Robb said, "I think the instincts of Governors Warner and Baliles, that the absence of Governor Wilder's support would be the story, are correct. I didn't realize he still hadn't signed on. Unfortunately, I don't have any special way to contact Governor Wilder, but I think it does make sense to hold off until you do."

For months, the requirement that Wilder participate had never even been hinted at by Baliles, Holton, or Robb. Warner had joked with me about never knowing what Wilder will do, but the governor never said the joint statement would be a no-go without him.

Robb, at least, offered this bit of encouragement: "Hang in there. Your additional patience will be rewarded."

Minute by minute, however, the 2004 session of the Virginia General Assembly was passing us by.

I believed that even Wilder's lack of participation in the joint statement would prove positive in the end because it would attract more attention to the *Brown* Scholarships. If Wilder's refusal to sign on made the headline larger, or gave us a second story with an additional headline, I thought that would ultimately help, especially with the media, the governor, and the legislators focused on the commonwealth's fiscal problems and the surrounding political trench warfare. The more publicity, the harder it would be for the General Assembly to defeat our legislation. The only thing that would jeopardize the headline was if we killed it ourselves.

I was certain the joint statement had to be issued or the funding war would be lost. Everything depended on this public declaration of support, with or without Wilder.

Nobody ever said a joint statement lacking the signature of Virginia's only African American governor would look particularly suspect. But I wondered if that was in the back of their minds. Whatever happened with Wilder, I believed, it was time for governors to act like governors. Waiting until the legislation was defeated to see if Wilder might sign on to a joint statement would achieve nothing. A funeral is no time to administer CPR to what has become a corpse in a casket.

FINALLY, EIGHT MONTHS AFTER I began trying to contact Wilder, his office asked for my fax number. On Groundhog Day 2004, I saw something shadow-like—a copy of an email Doug Wilder had sent to Ellen Qualls. I was getting closer to him, because he told his office to fax the copy to me:

Dear Ellen, as you know, Ken Woodley has been in communication with my office . . . about a bill that the governor says he is interested in. I was told, however, that the governor had not put any money in the budget for it. You and I have had experience with these kinds of things. Recognizing that he must have had his reasons, it would be helpful to know what they were before getting back to Mr. Woodley."

Though glad for the contact from Wilder, I was concerned that he might believe no thought had been given to funding the scholarships. I faxed him an explanation of the two-pronged strategy, noting that a $2 million budget amendment was pending in both the House and Senate. Sticking up for Warner, I told Wilder the governor had pledged to fight with us.

I believed there was no way that Mark Warner would not fight for funding, and I wanted Wilder to be clear on that critical point. But I wished Warner would speak for himself. Baliles sounded as frustrated as I was: "Can't Warner's office communicate that to Wilder themselves?"

I NEEDED TO COMMUNICATE with Governor Warner personally and I did so. I called Warner's special advisor, Rich Williams, who said that if I faxed a letter he would make sure it reached the governor. Here's the February 3 letter [emphasis in the original]:

The people of Prince Edward County who had their educations stolen during massive resistance need you to act on your heart and the words you spoke to me on May 8, 2003 and January 22, 2004. They need you to stand up for state funding for House Bill 846 and Senate Bill 230. On May 8, as our group discussed funding for this legislation you finally turned to me at the end of the meeting—I was sitting to your immediate left—and said, *"I will fight with you on this."* And I believed you. As I still believe you. On January 22, last month, as I told you of the former governors I had lined up to support this legislation, you told me, as we walked toward the governor's mansion, *"If it's a number that I can live with, then I'd love to do it in concert with the other governors and let it get attention from everybody."* And I believed you. As I still believe you.

There is a budget amendment of $2 million in the House and Senate. The public will support your stand because that amount roughly equals what the state would have spent educating these families between 1959–64. In 1958 the state spent $369,000 on public education in Prince Edward. Multiply that by five years. Also, those same people continued to pay state taxes during those five years. This should be viewed not solely in the context of the present budget but, accurately, and historically, as unfinished business. Appropriate the money now for these same people. It is a one-time debt of honor . . . Just do this one great thing now for these people who won the right of a public education for all Americans and lost their own. We need to give it back to them.

I did not receive a reply from Warner but Wilder's office called and asked for my email address. My adrenaline was flowing: Something was coming.

When I got home from work, my wife told me that Ellen Qualls had telephoned and wanted me to call her back. Qualls had never called me at home. When I reached her, she said a "worst-case scenario" had developed—it had become "a pissing match with Doug Wilder."

That did not surprise me. Politically speaking, zippers had been down for a while. But what she said next stunned me.

Qualls said Warner had received the letter I'd faxed earlier in the day and had responded that he had not meant state funding during a budget crisis, and that he was still looking for information on the number of people affected by massive resistance.

I was staggered. I felt the governor had abandoned his *Brown* Scholarship pledge.

Qualls added that there had been some thought of Warner coming out with a solo statement, but even that might now "draw some fire from Wilder" as too little too late.

With Wilder, she concluded, "everything turns to shit."

After trying to reach him since the spring of 2003, the transmission of Wilder's first direct communication to me came indirectly via a third party. Qualls was good enough to forward Wilder's email after recognizing that he'd tried to email it to me as well but had made a mistake with my address.

Wilder's February 3 email read:

The enclosed email from Ms. Qualls makes the situation crystal clear, at least in my judgment. Apparently, the governor believes we have hundreds of millions of dollars available to cut the estate taxes of the wealthiest citizens in Virginia, but not one dollar to do what you say he supports. I have written recently on this perceived level of unfair tax burdens for those at the bottom rung to be sacrificed for the benefit of the more affluent.

It will soon be fifty years since a Virginia governor was too busy with other things to look out for the school children in your area and other parts of the commonwealth.

Except for soothing empty words, nothing appears to have fundamentally changed.

As you may know, I will be speaking at the commemorative anniversary of the school closing period in April.

Right now, my agreeing to the press release being drafted by the Governor would suggest I approve of this.

I do not. If my lack of participation requires some further explanation I will be obliged to do so.

Sincerely, Doug Wilder.

cc Ellen Qualls

BUT THE "ENCLOSED EMAIL from Ms. Qualls" had not been included by Qualls in her forward of Wilder's email to me. I didn't like any of my guesses at what was "crystal clear" to Wilder.

I wasted no time in responding to Wilder's email. Clearly, Wilder felt as strongly as I did about the money. Scholarships that weren't grants-in-aid would be a fraud. But there was that $2 million budget amendment in the House and Senate. I emailed Wilder asking if he would publicly support those two funding pieces for the scholarships, coupled with HB 846 and SB 230, which would create the *Brown v. Board of Education* Scholarship Program that the budget amendments would fund. And I wanted him to send me that mysterious "enclosed email from Ms. Qualls."

Desperation had set in and I was scrambling to break through the joint-statement gridlock. Baliles said there was reason for concern if we didn't get the joint statement out in good time. He was preaching to the choir, the acolytes, the organist, and the preacher.

Then Baliles and I took the joint-statement strategy in a crucial direction. Responding to my comment that Wilder didn't want to be part of a statement that didn't specify funding, Baliles suggested the phrase "a sum sufficient" be added to the statement. I countered, during our February 4 conversation, by saying the joint statement should express support for the $2 million budget amendments as part of the governors' endorsement of HB 846 and SB 230. Doing so, he agreed, was a no-brainer. The two of us found common ground on the phrase "a sum sufficient not to exceed $2 million," and Baliles said I should email Qualls with that suggested addition to the statement.

"Don't panic," he told me, adding that because it was so late in the game we might want to time the joint statement's release for the day the legislation went to conference committee, if—and the words cut right through me—we're certain the *Brown* Scholarships will make it as far as the conferees.

That same day I received an email directly from Wilder. The subject line was: "Ahh . . . the money."

Wilder had sent me a copy of the February 2 email from Qualls that had made things so "crystal clear" that he would have nothing to do with the joint statement as worded at that time. Reading what Qualls had told Wilder, I understood perfectly:

> . . . State funding to seed the scholarship fund is not in the Governor's budget and he is currently not proposing it. We've got this little tax debate going on down here that I know you don't think highly of. So we've tried not to create "new spending items" as much as possible in this context.
>
> This does not rule out the possibility of state funding at a future time. Can you be supportive of this concept without a funding commitment? And if so, do you desire any edits to the statement?

No wonder Wilder had refused to sign on.

Seeing the administration declare in writing that Warner was not currently proposing any funding for the *Brown* Scholarships deepened my disappointment and anger. Frankly, I felt betrayed.

On February 6, I faxed Baliles a long letter, still convinced the joint-statement battle absolutely must be won for state-funded *Brown* Scholarships to have any chance in a General Assembly vote during the 2004 session.

> The bottom line first: it may be necessary for you and Governors Holton and Robb to issue your own joint statement in support of the legislation and the $2 million budget amendments . . . If Mr. Warner is unprepared to lead, he may need to follow you. I cannot abandon these people but my voice is not loud enough to command the necessary attention. . . .
>
> . . . Worst-case scenario if Governor Wilder doesn't join you? After being so emotional about a lack of funding in the previous statement, how can he credibly criticize anyone's support of the entire budget amendment sought by two African American legislators on the legislation's behalf? In Vietnam, the military said it was necessary to destroy the village in order to save it. Even if someone tries to step on this headline, it is better to get the headline out there to do what good it can rather than never do the good thing. Let's not destroy the headline ourselves in order to save it. That allows the wrong side to win and the losers have already been robbed of educational opportunity once already. Not a second time.

Baliles responded with words I had been praying to hear. "It seems to me that we just say we're going to release it. Let's assume Wilder doesn't say anything, or agree, then we're going ahead and release it by the three governors . . . We'll shoot for one day next week, and let the others know if they want to be on board they can."

Next week meant the joint statement would be issued a month into the session that had convened on January 14, but it would also mean it was finally issued and could achieve whatever good was still possible.

"It would guarantee," I told Baliles, "we had done all we could."

"That's right," he agreed.

ANSWERING THE PHONE ON February 6, I discovered the voice at the other end of the line belonged to former Virginia Governor L. Douglas Wilder. After months of frustration and exasperation, the moment had finally come: our first conversation.

Wilder would have absolutely nothing to do with the joint statement without Warner's total funding commitment.

"I don't intend to be part of another cruel hoax on the people," he said, adding that the state of Virginia can't recognize "this is not even a spit in the mud" and all the while it plans to give estate tax breaks "to millionaires" and spend $30 million for an arts center in downtown Richmond.

"Take $2 million off of that," Wilder said, the emotion in his voice making his words sound like ricochets off stone. "Damn right . . . the buck stops with the governor," he added. "It's meritorious what you're trying to do, but the governor could put it in the budget."

I knew that Wilder was correct. My hope was that on veto day the governor would ensure that there was $2 million for the scholarships—this year, budget crisis or no budget crisis—if the General Assembly had not already done so.

"When is he going to fight with you?" Wilder asked.

I had no answer to a question I had been asking myself for weeks, and I told Wilder that I felt I had been betrayed.

"You have been," he agreed.

Everything was up to the present occupant of the Executive Mansion. Wilder said he remained ready to support Warner's support of funding for the scholarships. That was Wilder's phrase—he would support the governor's support.

"If the governor supports it with funding," Wilder reiterated, "I'll be the first there . . . I'll be the first to say I support it."

When I told him "I shouldn't have to be doing all this," Wilder replied, "You've done a helluva job. I'm proud of you. It's laudable, good."

Wilder said that I shouldn't even have to "mess with" the Senate Finance Committee. "The governor could amend his budget any time he wanted and then let the people vote to overturn it, up or down." He also wanted to know why the scholarship proposal was split into two different pieces. "Why didn't the governor put it in his budget himself?"

Wilder then observed, "Everybody says Wilder is the fly in the ointment. I'm not the fly in the ointment."

My encounters with Wilder would leave me feeling that he was far more like a spider poised on its web, watching frightened moths blowing helplessly toward it in the wind.

I asked Wilder directly if he would join former governors Baliles, Robb, and Holton in supporting the $2 million budget amendment, along with the scholarship program. Wilder told me I could tell the governor's office that he would support the governor's support.

"When the governor's office gets behind it is when I'll get behind it," Wilder said. "I'm not interested in talk, not interested in platitudes. I'm interested in money."

And then we said goodbye.

When I told him of my long-awaited conversation with Wilder, Baliles said, "He drives a hard bargain, doesn't he?"

He does indeed, I admitted.

Call Qualls, Baliles advised, after asking if she would accept my call. "If I tell her I just spoke with Wilder," I predicted, "she'll take my call."

February 6 then became truly surreal. A former governor of Virginia authorized me to issue what amounted to an ultimatum to the current governor on behalf of himself and two other former governors. Baliles instructed me to tell Qualls that he, Robb, and Holton would issue their own statement—even without Wilder, if they must—by midweek in support of the legislation and the money to make the scholarships real. And they'd leave the current governor in their wake if he did not come aboard.

"I think we have a breakthrough," I told Qualls, velvet-gloving the uppercut that was on its way, "an opening." And then I delivered the ultimatum.

Before leaving for home at the end of the day, I sent Qualls an email that put on the record the "with-or-without-Governor Warner" declaration.

I could not imagine Mark Warner choosing "without."

The legislative window of opportunity was lowering rapidly. On February 11, a Wednesday, we were just six days from "crossover" day. Both the House and Senate needed to finish their work so their respective bills could be sent for consideration by the other chamber. Any bills not ready for crossover were well and truly finished.

The timing also meant the joint statement absolutely had to be released this week to have any impact on what remained of the legislative session. At the very least, the words might influence the conference committee's final budget decisions, and, if one proved necessary, a budget amendment from the governor, if he would do so, for the veto day session.

Responding to a fax, Wilder called me for a second time but didn't react favorably to a redrafted joint statement. "In essence," he said, "it says the same thing."

No, I replied, this time the statement supports the $2 million budget amendment, too.

"That's not good enough for me," Wilder replied, and he counseled, "we'll get it but we've got to keep the pressure on." Wilder told me he still wanted Warner to say he intended to put the funding in the budget. "I'll have him put it in, or wish he had . . . I've been around this game. If he thought so much of" the scholarship program he would put the money in the budget.

Of Warner's reluctance to do so, Wilder observed, "he's not doing us any damn favors . . . He could call up his good friend John Chichester and say, 'John, I've got to have this or I'm not going to be able to stay in town.' And Warner won't be able to stay in town."

Senate Finance Committee Chairman Chichester was Warner's key Republican ally in the Senate. Chairmanship of the Senate Finance Committee is a position of great power and Chichester had agreed with Warner's call to raise revenue as part of a comprehensive economic package to address the fiscal debacle.

"They don't give a goddamn . . . They know the game . . . They've been governors," Wilder said (apparently targeting, and unfairly, in my opinion, Baliles, Robb, and Holton). Everyone who signs on to the joint statement, he continued, could say, after funding for the scholarships failed, "'Well, I supported it.' But did they really? It's still a word game," he declared.

There was no long wait for Wilder to confirm his decision.

He sent me a copy of his next email to Qualls:

In view of what seems to have transpired, and what the possibilities are as to achieving the desired results, I feel a separate statement from me would be more appropriate—many thanks, Doug."

I wasn't surprised. In fact, I'd eventually concluded that Wilder might prove most effective as a solo agent. "I want you to be true to yourself. Doug Wilder is a valuable teammate, your unique qualities pushing fiercely . . . You must make the decision you feel is in the best interest of helping this legislation pass with funding," I'd told him in an email. The threat of Wilder as a "nemesis" factor, I came to believe, would encourage Warner to pursue full funding for the reparation scholarships. It was a role that Wilder could, and would, play well.

Friday the 13th—an appropriate date—began with Governor Warner's participation in the joint statement still not assured. Qualls told me she'd not yet spoken to the governor but would be traveling with him today.

As far as I was concerned, push had come to shove as hard as we can.

I called Baliles's office and left a message for him to call me. He did, and the man I had leaned upon most was proving himself able to bear the weight. There would be no more delays. The thing was simply going to be done today.

Baliles said he had already clearly informed Qualls that he, Robb, and Holton were releasing a statement of support before lunch. Warner then signed on to the joint statement, Baliles said, and Qualls told the governor's office to release it statewide at noon. No ifs. No buts.

That's what happens when three former governors deliver their own ultimatum. The administration had dragged its heels when I delivered the Baliles-Robb-Holton release-the-statement-or-else message. The governor-to-governor delivery got those feet moving as if they were walking barefoot over hot coals. Which, I suppose, they were.

Baliles asked me about Wilder and Allen and advised me to wait until the joint statement was "out on the wire" before contacting them. Gilmore, too, he told me.

When I told Baliles that he was "the true-blue one," and that I honored him for standing up—not with me but with the people we were fighting for—he replied: "It was worth it."

Later he recalled his ultimatum-delivering phone call this way: "I remember the call to the third floor [the governor's office at the Capitol], saying, 'We're coming out with it at 11 o'clock, come hell or high water.' And their response: 'Can you delay it a little bit?'"

Only until lunch.

Thus, a few minutes after noon I received the call I'd been waiting for.

The joint statement, Qualls told me, is going out—she paused and said—"going out now," as the "send" button was pressed while I was on the phone with her. A copy was being sent to my home email as well as to the fax machine in the *Farmville Herald*'s newsroom.

I thanked her and asked her to express my gratitude to the governor.

Qualls said, "We'll talk."

"Still friends?"

Yes, she said, laughing, "still friends."

The weeks of back-and-forth emails and phone calls hadn't been easy for either of us. At one point I told her, "I know I'm a pain in the ass," and she'd quickly replied, "Yes, you are." I had to be.

The joint statement emerged from the *Herald*'s fax machine at ten past noon:

> Governor Mark R. Warner and three former Virginia governors today released a joint statement in support of the passage and funding of House Bill 846 and Senate Bill 230, creating a *Brown v. Board of Education* Scholarship Program and Fund, to be established for the purpose of providing specific educational opportunities for families denied a public education during massive resistance.

The release quoted the four governors declaring:

> We particularly focus on the students of Prince Edward County who, led by 16-year-old Barbara Johns, helped win the end of segregation in America's public schools through their crucial involvement in the 1954

Brown v. Board decision, then lost their own educational opportunity when public schools were closed for five years during the massive resistance response to *Brown* before finally winning, in the Supreme Court's 1964 *Griffin v. Prince Edward* decision, the constitutional right of every American child to a public education.

We believe it is singularly appropriate to give educational opportunity and the promise of prosperity and enrichment it offers to those families and individuals who were denied it by an egregious public policy.

On the 50th anniversary of *Brown v. Board* and the 40th anniversary of *Griffin v. Prince Edward*, we signal our bipartisan support of this effort and of the expression of regret contained in the legislation.

We further believe that the scholarship program should be funded during the biennium with a sum sufficient, not to exceed $2 million, in order to establish, administer, and begin the implementation of the scholarship program.

Weeks of frustration and anger suddenly seemed like a distant memory. But I felt certain that without Baliles, Holton, and Robb that joint statement never would have been released.

Former Governor Holton responded to my thanks for his joint-statement stand, writing, "Thanks and congratulations for getting it this far. Without you, it would have been long dead."

In expressing my gratitude to former Governor Robb for his support with the joint statement, I told him, "It was a very wonderful thing to walk through the woods at sunset and see the reflection of the sky in the small Appomattox River where the Civil War ended and to know that there are such men left who do stand up for people and principles and bring a bit of the sky to earth, so to speak. I know passage is not guaranteed but we have not, and will not, leave any muscle of mind or body unused. Sometimes one must turn the reflections into landscapes."

Robb's emailed response came quickly: "Your poetic prose, not to mention your dogged determination, make my day!"

I KNEW THAT THIS muster of governors would not be too little. I still had faith that it would not be too late. I called Mike Thomas, chief of staff at Senator Allen's office, as promised, and then the offices of Wilder and Gilmore. Allen had decided not to join his gubernatorial colleagues in their explicit call for state funds. True to his word, however, Allen issued a strong statement of support that implied state funding. I was grateful to both Thomas and Allen for the response.

"Wrongful, cold-hearted, and racist attitudes led to the deplorable policy of massive resistance," the senator declared, adding that "there is no doubt that the policies of massive resistance had long-lasting negative effects on the lives of thousands of Virginians. . . . Although it may be fifty years since the policy of massive resistance denied a 'lost generation' of its citizens a public education it is altogether appropriate that we provide them with the education they deserve."

The Associated Press noted the absence of Wilder and quoted his condemnation of the joint statement, which stung even though I knew it was coming. The General Assembly might yet turn the prayed-for promise of the legislation into a cruel hoax, but the words and intention of the governors in the joint statement were anything but.

As for Gilmore, the AP story noted his questions over funding the scholarships but reported his basic support of the idea. The *Brown* Scholarships could live with that. Gilmore and I had communicated on several occasions about his possible participation in the joint statement. His last email had authorized me to add his name to the joint statement. But Gilmore's decision was based on his understanding that the General Assembly had specified the scholarships would be privately funded. I could not in good conscience, therefore, tell Qualls to add his name to a public statement supporting $2 million in state funds.

As newspaper coverage would demonstrate, the joint statement's impact was not diminished by Wilder's nonparticipation. We had a headline and it spoke for itself, with power.

Jeff Schapiro's story led the *Richmond Times-Dispatch*'s General Assembly coverage in the February 14 edition. The headline read: "Governors regret past 'egregious' policy,'" and Schapiro's lead paragraph reported that "Governor Mark R. Warner and three of his predecessors—two Democrats and a Republican—are urging the GOP-controlled General Assembly to support scholarships for black Virginians denied an education during 'massive resistance' to court-ordered school desegregation."

Three days later, the paper had an item on Allen's endorsement.

The stories and headlines provided political support for the *Brown* Scholarships in the remaining days of the regular 2004 session, but they also laid the foundation for the endgame strategy, if needed, in the upcoming one-day veto session.

THE JOINT STATEMENT PAID off immediately.

"ABC World News Tonight" was on the line and a crucial phone call from the *Washington Post* was just days away.

The United States of America was beginning to pay attention. Hell or high water had won the day.

8

Wings For a Prayer

The February 25 telephone call from Jo Becker of the *Washington Post* felt like the hand of fate giving us its grip. I held on tight.

In the course of her interview, Becker asked about Warner and his commitment to me, and the contradiction of his not putting any money for the scholarships in the state budget. I seized the moment and replied that funding would come down to a Warner budget amendment on veto day. Becker then asked the $2 million question—was I going to ask the governor to do so? I provided the $2 million answer: Yes, I told her, I was.

And I did.

Immediately after speaking with Becker I wrote and faxed a letter to the governor asking him to send down a budget amendment for the veto session if the conferees didn't increase funding. I wanted what I had told Becker—and what I hoped she'd report—to be the absolute truth without a moment's delay.

I told Warner:

> History is going to be left in your hands. It appears almost certain that you will have the final say regarding funding for the *Brown v. Board of Education* Scholarship Program and Fund. Both the House and Senate have unanimously passed the legislation but, hypocritically, the House hasn't included a penny of funding and the Senate only has $100,000. The original budget amendment in the House and Senate was for $2 million. And it is sufficient funding up to that amount which you and

former Governors Baliles, Holton and Robb so importantly endorsed in the February 13 joint statement issued by your office.

You have the authority to propose a budget amendment for the General Assembly to consider during the veto session. Please, sir, do so if the conference committee does not increase funding. There can be a sunset clause so that if we are all wrong and there is not sufficient demand for the scholarship program the money returns to the treasury . . . You have the support to make this history. The people of Prince Edward will come to Richmond and stand beside you.

Acting on the advice I'd received from former Governor Allen's counsel, Frank B. Atkinson, I told Warner:

The conference committee may be persuaded to appropriate the $2 million were you to go back channel to them first. The conferees can constitutionally and procedurally increase funding if they agree, by their rules, to do so. But the General Assembly has so far hidden in cover over the funding. If you send down a budget amendment, and turn your words of February 13 into history, there will not be enough legislators willing to be held publicly accountable for overriding your budget amendment and turning massive resistance into Dismissive Assistance.

There is generally an unappropriated balance in the budget where funding might come from, and it is my understanding that you are not legally bound to offer a parallel cut, though in a $59 billion budget there must be room for this debt of honor that is neither new funding nor a new program. The state has had these funds since 1959–1964.

You have the fate of this funding, and this redemptive moment in Virginia's history, in your hands. Please send the budget amendment to the General Assembly when the time comes. We're with you.

I called the ever-dependable Rich Williams, special advisor to the governor. He promised to make certain Warner got the letter. Becker called back that afternoon to fact-check her story and to confirm that I was calling on Warner to send down his own $2 million budget amendment for the veto session. I told her that I had made it a formal request in writing and that Warner's office had assured me it would be placed in the governor's hands.

One of the most important days of the *Brown* Scholarship crusade became still more pivotal when Senator Marsh called me at home that night. Yes, Marsh told me, he would introduce a last-minute amendment the following day for $1.95 million to make it a full $2 million. He had read my letter and then run to the senate clerk's office to do the late filing.

Marsh assured me he would take the fight to the floor of the Senate. Senator Lambert had no objection, Marsh told me, but didn't think the intervention would succeed.

"People don't understand the importance of this legislation," Marsh said.

I told the senator about my formal request to Warner for a veto session budget amendment if all else failed, and Marsh offered the encouraging thought that taking the fight to the Senate floor, having a record of the battle prior to veto day, would help the governor do so.

The next morning, I read Becker's story in the *Washington Post*'s February 26 online edition. The sun had not yet risen, but there was a feeling of light all around.

In the middle of the *Post* story was the paragraph that changed everything and provided real hope for ultimate victory, even if the Senate stuck to its $100,000.

Becker reported my plea to Warner to send legislators a budget amendment that would fully fund the scholarships. She put it right out there for all to see. Most importantly, she wrote that press secretary Ellen Qualls said the governor would do just that if legislators did not during the regular session.

At that moment, I was certain—no matter how long and tortuous the remaining journey—the *Brown* Scholarships would have a fund totaling $2 million.

How significant was Becker's phone call?

It had taken weeks of mini-operatic struggle to get Warner to agree to a joint statement, minus Wilder, in support of the scholarships and calling for funding of up to $2 million to make them real: that much work to generate support for someone *else's* budget amendment.

How long it would take to secure the governor's commitment to offer his *own* $2 million budget amendment for veto day—new funding during a budget crisis—was something I tried not to think about in the small, dark hours of a winter's night. I tried to count sheep to fall asleep, not the number of times I might have had to harass Ellen Qualls.

But thanks to Becker's story it took less than 24 hours and was on the record for everyone to see. Becker had given my budget amendment request to Warner the leverage it needed.

When I reached my office and turned to the *Richmond Times-Dispatch's* General Assembly coverage, my elation grew. Unsurprisingly, Jeff Schapiro had learned of this critically important development, too, and had written an entire article under the headline "Warner asks for education funding" and had this subhead: "He urges $2 million in scholarships for those denied school."

Schapiro's story quoted Kevin Hall, Warner's deputy press secretary, saying the governor "thinks this is a significant and reasonable gesture on the part of the commonwealth." Hall added that it was appropriate, "especially this year" as the fiftieth anniversary of the *Brown* decision approached.

The joint statement by Warner, Baliles, Robb, and Holton was referenced in the article, and it was noted that Allen and Gilmore had indicated their support. Schapiro also pointed out Wilder's insistence on funding.

Each and every governor, in his own way, had supported the *Brown v. Board of Education* Scholarships, which meant money to make them real, just as I had hoped for as we struggled to get that joint statement released.

For the *Farmville Herald's* story on Warner's budget amendment commitment I had, of course, wanted a direct statement to the paper of record for Prince Edward County rather than an administration comment quoted, with attribution, from another newspaper. My deadline was pushed up because I was going to Richmond to meet with Senator Marsh and watch him take the fight to the floor of the Senate. That meant calling Qualls at 7:30 a.m.

Qualls understood, of course, after I explained, and told me "the governor believes that the fiftieth anniversary of the landmark *Brown v. Board* decision is a particularly appropriate time to provide educational opportunity for people denied it by an egregious state policy." I thanked her and she replied, "Good luck."

Before making an early morning drive to the Capitol with Rita Moseley, I made sure Qualls's words would appear in the *Farmville Herald* that day and I faxed my thanks to Governor Warner. With a black Magic Marker, I printed the word "Beautiful!" in three-inch-high letters, underlining the letters. Beneath it I taped the paragraph from the *Washington Post* containing Qualls's declaration of his budget amendment commitment in response to my request. As always, Rich Williams promised to make certain the governor received my fax.

VETO DAY WOULD NEVER be easy. The scholarship crusade had been a harrowing journey through a political minefield and I was not starry-eyed enough to think I would suddenly find myself at Disney World with the General Assembly singing "It's a small world after all." But I had absolute faith in our ultimate success. If we did the work. If we reached out with aggressive affection to the GOP. And took nothing for granted.

If all that were to be done, there was no way the General Assembly would defeat a specific budget amendment from the governor.

Not on veto day. Not on public display with no political cover as the nation celebrated the fiftieth anniversary of the *Brown* decision.

But, until veto day came—it was scheduled for April 21—the General Assembly would prove there was no turn it would not twist and no twist it could not turn.

9

The Eye of the Storm

Political winds that a hurricane would envy were howling at the *Brown* Scholarships in both chambers of the Virginia General Assembly. But Senator Marsh had a simple, last-minute plan to fully fund the scholarships without adding a penny to the proposed Senate budget—take $950,000 a year from the pot of Student Financial Aid Assistance funding already in the budget. With the $50,000 the Senate was already proposing for each year of the two-year budget, the scholarship program would then be fully funded at $2 million.

Marsh briefed Rita Moseley and me on the plan in his Senate office prior to the February 26 legislative session. Using state monies intended for student financial aid to fund the *Brown* Scholarships was simple and appropriate, a glass slipper we hoped would fit.

As part of his strategy, Marsh had placed a copy of Jo Becker's *Washington Post* story on the desk of every senator, making clear the growing media interest in the reparation's fate. Becker had also interviewed John Hurt. Anyone who did not live through those five years of massive resistance in Prince Edward County—and their lifetime of consequences—can only begin to understand. But they should certainly try. Becker's story gave them a chance to do so.

Denying the continued fallout from massive resistance by saying it happened forty-five years ago wouldn't make its radioactivity go away. I hoped that as they listened to what Marsh was going to say that morning senators would acknowledge a reality that existed nowhere else on Earth.

Marsh, at least, understood.

On the floor of the Senate, Marsh said it would be "tragic indeed, a tragedy on a tragedy" if the full $2 million was not approved. A scholarship program established by a General Assembly that then refused to fund the scholarships would be a travesty, he stressed at the outset of a dramatic scene that I would recount in the *Farmville Herald*.

Moseley and I watched from the Senate gallery as Marsh declared that funding the scholarships is "the fair thing to do, the right thing to do."

Marsh reminded his Senate colleagues that they had passed the legislation creating the scholarship program by a 40–0 vote, as the House had by a 99–0 vote. The $2 million, he continued, seizing on the talking point I'd provided, virtually equals the amount the state would have appropriated for public education in the county had schools not closed in Prince Edward County.

As for accessible use of the scholarships, Farmville's Longwood University, and Southside Virginia Community College, a twenty-minute drive away, could provide that opportunity, Marsh noted.

Despite his best efforts, Marsh's words were having no effect.

Senate Finance Committee Chairman John Chichester defended the $50,000 for each of the budget's two years. "I don't know of a finance committee member who's not sympathetic to this," he said, explaining that the problem was that nobody knew how many people would step forward to take advantage of the scholarships.

I was sitting next to someone who would apply for a scholarship, and I wondered what must be going through Moseley's mind.

Chichester said the Senate Finance Committee would be willing to increase funding back the following year beyond the $50,000 should the scholarship applications justify doing so.

There had been so many political twists in the *Brown* Scholarship crusade that it made the game of Twister look like chiropractor-prescribed therapy to straighten the spine. Though I thought we'd seen everything, neither Moseley nor I were prepared for the drama unfolding below us on the Senate floor. We watched and listened as Lambert, our Senate patron, stood and argued against—that's right, *against*—Marsh's budget amendment to fully fund the scholarship program created by Lambert's own bill.

Lambert agreed with Chichester that there was a problem ascertaining how many potential students there were, particularly because the target students were in a nontraditional student population. The Senate wanted to help them, he said, describing the $50,000 as a "place-holder" until the number of scholarship applicants could be determined. Lambert echoed Chichester that more money could be added next year.

Marsh countered that "we can provide this information." I had given him a copy of Edward H. Peeples's study on the number of black and (substantially fewer) white children whose educations had been permanently affected by massive resistance. No, we didn't know how many people would use a scholarship, but we did know the size of the potential applicant pool. I had included that information in the February 24 letter I faxed to Lambert's office. This was enough to know, in my opinion, that $50,000 was simply not enough to create a functional scholarship program.

"The funds are available," Marsh added, asking the chairman if it were true that $75 million had been set up for student financial aid in the state. Chichester replied that he could not remember the precise amount, but because Marsh had asked the question, the senator must have checked for himself and knew it to be true. "So yes," Chichester responded.

Marsh then pressed the point that it was "appropriate to use a small portion of that funding for these students and *their* higher education."

But that $75 million, Chichester responded, addressed only about 35 percent of the current need. He repeated that "we don't know how many folks would take advantage" of the scholarship funding and "setting aside $2 million in that case would not be the best use of a dollar." He repeated that if it was clear next year there was a need for more *Brown* Scholarship funds, "every member" would want to increase the appropriation.

Observing all this, I could only feel that waiting one more year—for people who had waited too long already and were in their fifties and sixties—was not the answer. Nor would a $50,000 scholarship fund, slashed as everyone would know from $2 million, be persuasive that the scholarship program was more than the "cruel hoax" Wilder had warned about.

Marsh was trying his best, but it was difficult to overcome opposition when it came from the bill's own Senate patron.

Lambert said, "I thank the chairman for the [$50,000] he did provide." He pledged again that the finance committee would find more funding once the number of students was known.

And then it was over.

On a voice vote, the Senate sustained the $50,000 for each year of the biennium budget. No vote, therefore, was specifically taken on Senator Marsh's last-minute budget amendment.

But Marsh was not over and he was not out.

"The fight," he assured Moseley and me, "is just beginning."

It was "all too easy" for the scholarships "to be lost in the confusion of the budget" battle, Marsh said, therefore the issue needed to be projected further out into the public domain.

A plan to do just that had come to me as the debate between Marsh, Lambert, and Chichester played out on the Senate floor: we needed to stage a rally, bring "a sea of humanity" from Prince Edward County to the Capitol. Not just a press conference, but a full-fledged event that could not be ignored—a gathering that would persuade the House and Senate that full funding of $2 million was justified. "We'll answer the Senate's question," I promised Marsh, "about who might use the scholarships."

With a rally on veto day, we would see to it that legislators had to walk through the answer on their way to deciding the fate of the budget amendment from Warner that looked to be our only hope.

LAMBERT HAD MADE VIRGINIA political history when he became the first African American appointed to the powerful Senate Finance Committee. I knew he faced competing pressure from both sides of the political aisle. I also understood that to be an effective Democratic member of a GOP-controlled finance committee, he could not adopt a series of contrary positions without inevitably isolating himself from the majority and seriously weakening his position. And he could always be removed from the finance committee and appointed instead to some less powerful committee. As wiser men than I have rightfully observed, politics is the art of compromise and achieving what is possible. I had just thought far more was possible. But I had to remind myself that in the House of Delegates, no funds at all had been possible.

Further, while writing this book I came to understand and appreciate that $100,000 was truly all that Lambert could get out of the Senate during the 2004 regular legislative session. According to one of his state government confidantes, Lambert lamented the amount and was "very disappointed" that the General Assembly did not fully fund the scholarship program—he felt fortunate to have gotten *any* money for the scholarships.

Reassessing in hindsight the funding amendment in the Senate Finance Committee in February of 2004, I had to rethink my angry reaction to Lambert's support of that $100,000 rather than the full $2 million. The senator is deceased and I cannot ask him about the rationale for his support. Nor can he defend himself.

Had Lambert reacted toward his fellow Senate Finance Committee members with the anger that I felt, his colleagues might have walked away from what some regarded as very controversial *Brown* Scholarships. Instead, Lambert got what funding he could, knowing that he could come back for more later.

I called John Stokes after Moseley and I returned from Richmond. I told him we needed to organize two hundred people to come from Prince Edward County on veto day and make the General Assembly members walk through a sea of humanity—"touching the wounds"—on their way from the General Assembly building to the Capitol. Given my many responsibilities as editor of the *Farmville Herald* and the need to maintain direct engagement with the governor's office and members of the General Assembly, there were days when it felt like even my fumes were running on fumes. I knew I could never organize the truly effective showing we so desperately needed.

But I knew that Stokes—one of Barbara Rose Johns's lieutenants in the 1951 student strike at Robert R. Moton High School—could. As we spoke, his enthusiasm kindled into flame on the spot.

Over the next few weeks, Stokes showed magnificent leadership in creating a local committee to organize turnout for the April 21 veto day.

When we spoke on March 3, Stokes told me he had talked to "people who are wounded and are coming out fighting."

Stokes and I agreed we would never be at this crossroads in history again. "This reminds me of 1951," Stokes enthused, thinking back to the "Manhattan Project" planning for the student strike. "The people on the committee are very excited . . . I took your concept [of a sea of humanity] and ran with it."

Ran with it? He was doing three-minute miles.

Stokes's involvement also seemed to be having a positive impact on his own life, helping to heal his hurt over what massive resistance did to his people in Prince Edward County. "You've raised me to another level," Stokes told me. "My wife said, 'You've brought my husband back to life.'"

I was not alone in believing a spirit of more than mortal dimension was at work.

"They are singing your praises," Stokes told me, passing on what the black community was feeling. "And it was divine intervention that brought you here to this community. Thank God for that."

His words brought me to my knees. I was not exultant. I prayed for strength to continue and complete the mission. My dreams had never been this big.

Moseley said there was such tremendous excitement in the community that people were already calling her, asking for scholarship applications. So much for legislative doubts that the scholarships would be used.

When the Prince Edward County Public Schools offered to provide us with five buses and drivers, we knew the biggest hurdle—getting everybody to the Capitol and at the same time—had been cleared.

AN INSURMOUNTABLE OBSTACLE, HOWEVER, was about to rise in the House of Delegates.

On March 5, Baskerville told me she'd be introducing an "amendment in the nature of a substitute." She would try to put back into HB 846 everything the House of Delegates had taken out, which included phrasing that could make the children and grandchildren eligible for the scholarships, as I had originally planned.

Her plan seemed straightforward enough, and I saw no reason to worry.

Two days later, Baskerville called to elaborate on her new legislative strategy. The amendment substitute put back all the original language. When it got to the House floor, her hope was that amid the hectic turmoil of the final week of the regular session, the House GOP members would not have time to read it. The substitute restored the progeny clause and the word "appropriation."

Her intent was to slip the substitute through.

I told myself that if the delegates were too busy to read the amendments and substitutes that came before them it was their fault. I saw nothing wrong with her plan, believing it doubled our chances of getting something to the governor's desk. Baskerville's strategy was a desperate roll of the dice, one that I supported. Her commitment to the reparation scholarships had been and would remain unswerving.

The Senate had no problem with Baskerville's substitute. But the Senate had never had a problem with "appropriation," even if it was just $100,000 for the 2004–2006 fiscal years.

House members, on the other hand, had Jupiter-sized problems with Baskerville's maneuver, once they figured out what was going on. She had hoped nobody would notice. They did notice, and they did not like it one bit.

Prince Edward County Delegate Clarke Hogan subsequently told me there is "a code of honor that you trust each other" over explanations of amendments, that it is up to the delegate offering the amendment to be forthcoming. "If you don't," the Republican told me, "it's taken personally, and she flat-out didn't do that." He said what had happened "now made it 100 times harder" to get anything through the House.

A hundred times harder in conference committee. A hundred times harder on veto day.

Moving forward, I told Hogan, the key will be Republicans in the House looking beyond Baskerville and not taking political revenge on the casualties of massive resistance who had already suffered enough.

Flush the partisan politics, I told Hogan, and he agreed that, yes, it was important for House members to look beyond their anger at Baskerville.

The eyes of the nation will be on Virginia, I pointed out, reiterating my longstanding hope that Republicans and Democrats would join together and that "massive redemption would have everybody's fingerprints on it."

Hogan sounded doubtful. "Do you really believe that can happen?"

THE NEXT DAY I began what would become a nine-week push to reach out to Republicans, especially in the House. I wanted to encourage them to look beyond petty politics and see what the scholarships were about: to understand how this moment of redemption was waiting, with hopes and prayers, for them to make a healing dream come true.

To achieve that goal, it was critical for them to see that the *Brown* Scholarship legislation had not come from any politician or political party, but from an everyday Virginian. Making that clear, I hoped, would take the partisan bull's-eye off the legislation. This strategy was not based on any criticism of Baskerville on my part but on the partisan view that so many House Republicans seemed to have of my House sponsor.

Republicans also needed to look at their party's DNA. Many legislators were too young to know about it, but a Republican senator, Ted Dalton, had led the fight in the General Assembly against massive resistance in the 1950s. So the *Brown* Scholarships were in the GOP's blood. I didn't learn that piece of Virginia political history until I read Frank B. Atkinson's book, *The Dynamic Dominion: Realignment and the Rise of Virginia's Republican Party Since 1945*.

Atkinson wrote that Dalton foresaw that General Assembly approval of state tuition grants for use in private schools might lead some localities to abandon their public school systems. But his arguments in 1955 did not deter the Byrd Machine-led General Assembly. State tuition grants were used, for a time, for the all-white private school in Prince Edward County—another reason for the state's "profound regret" and another argument for full state funding for the *Brown* Scholarships.

Dalton had sought to make certain Virginia would not undermine the state constitution's guarantee of public education. Atkinson wrote that Dalton was told by General Assembly colleagues not to worry, that the future of public education would not be threatened. Four years later, of course, massive resistance destroyed public education in Prince Edward County.

WITH EACH PASSING MINUTE, I was appreciating Lambert and his contribution to the cause more and more. The $100,000 in Senate funding, I realized, was an insignificant budget target for those trying to cut spending. What mattered was getting the *Brown* Scholarships through the General Assembly and then established as a program that could receive state appropriations. Even the smallest sum would achieve that goal and facilitate Governor Warner's budget amendment on veto day. The $100,000 proposed by the Senate reminded me of one of my favorite childhood books, *The Little Engine That Could*. The money Senator Lambert had brought this far down the legislative track might be the little appropriation that could . . . or else.

Doug Wilder, meanwhile, was fulfilling his "nemesis" role. In a March 7 op-ed published by the *Richmond Times-Dispatch* under the headline "Why Not State Funds for *Brown* Scholarships?," the former governor questioned Warner's commitment to the reparation legislation. Wilder quoted the January emails from Warner's press secretary Ellen Qualls revealing that state funds for the scholarships were not included in Warner's budget, nor was he proposing any at that time.

Wilder wrote, "Ken Woodley, editor of the *Farmville Herald*, has been indefatigable in his efforts since February of last year to bring about an aura of healing and give real diplomas to those who had them stolen from them."

I then learned that I hadn't been the first to suggest doing so.

The *Times-Dispatch* interrupted Wilder's commentary with this statement in parenthesis: "A. Barton Hinkle, associate editor and senior editorial writer for the *Times-Dispatch* Editorial Pages, first proposed such a program in a column September 11, 2001."

I had no idea Hinkle had done so, but then I looked at the date and understood. Hinkle's column was published on the morning of the worst terrorist attack in U.S. history. His suggestion had been overwhelmed by 9–11.

"For Woodley," Wilder had continued, "words were not enough: State funding for the program was essential or it means nothing."

Warner was calling for state funds now, I knew, but I wasn't disappointed to have Wilder put him in a spotlight that could only strengthen the governor's resolve.

THE NEED TO VIGOROUSLY lobby the GOP in the build-up to veto day became emphatically clear on March 16. Delegate Leo Wardrup returned my call and declared that Baskerville's House bill had no chance of getting to the governor.

"Unfortunately," he told me, "it had nothing to do with politics but with the methods used by Baskerville . . . We told her that bill was not going to come out of the House. The problem was with misrepresentation on the floor, not partisan politics . . . You can't do that, even if it's deleterious to your bill."

Once a delegate's credibility is gone, he told me, "it's gone."

Wardrup added that House members knew that Lambert's bill had passed the Senate, another example of the important contribution Lambert was making to the *Brown* Scholarships. In other words, the GOP could exact its revenge on Baskerville without killing the scholarship program itself. Of course, the House did not see any money in its vision of the *Brown* Scholarships. That particular form of blindness with regard to the meaning of "scholarships" persisted. From my point of view, Baskerville had only done what she thought was necessary to overcome that blindness.

Furthermore, when I told Wardrup that Warner was going to send down a budget amendment for full state funding on veto day, the delegate's reply felt like a lead weight. "That probably won't happen," Wardrup ominously predicted.

Even the Senate, he noted, was reluctant to put in state dollars.

Baskerville reacted to the House defeat of her substitute by issuing a public statement blasting her GOP colleagues:

> House Republicans repeated their position that no state money should be appropriated to the *Brown v. Board of Education* Scholarship Program. Once again, certain Virginia leaders are making dubious history. They deny taxpayers access to educational opportunity just as it was denied under massive resistance. These citizens contribute to Virginia's economy and civic discourse, despite the state's five-year denial of their right to an education.
>
> We cannot right the wrongs of the past, but the *Brown v. Board of*

Education Scholarship Program could show the nation that 21st century Virginia seeks to occupy a different place in the history books. To deny the same citizens educational funding a second time is a stinging wrong for the commonwealth."

Whatever the state of her relationship with House Republicans and its impact on the legislative journey, Baskerville's energy and support had been crucial from the beginning. Her embrace of the *Brown* Scholarship crusade had given me a go-to person in the General Assembly on the very first day, February 18, 2003, and she was by my side as the session began in January 2004. That was vital to my confidence. By now, however, confidence was hard to find.

Baskerville described veto day as a "severe hurdle." She wasn't sure the governor's planned budget amendment would pass because of the "attitude" in the House.

THAT MEANT I JUST had to get through to House Speaker William J. Howell.

In Virginia, the speaker of the House of Delegates is considered the second most powerful person in state government, after the governor. Among the speaker's potent powers is the appointment of House committees and their chairmen. Nobody wants to get on the wrong side of the speaker.

Howell, a 1967 graduate of the University of Virginia law school, ascended to the speaker's chair following the resignation of fellow Republican Vance Wilkins in 2002. Wilkins had reveled in his power as speaker and was a combative politician, wielding the gavel like a hammer. Howell was chosen by his House colleagues because he would follow in Wilkins's footsteps without bringing those heavy-handed qualities to the position.

Howell was an estate lawyer who worked in a two-story log cabin on the banks of the Rappahannock River near Falmouth. In the Spring 2004 *UVA Lawyer,* Howell told writer Cullen Couch:

> Speaker wasn't something that I was seeking or ever had any inclination of wanting to do. I was really quite content with my lot in life prior to being Speaker. But when it became apparent that we were going to have

a new Speaker, of course I immediately began thinking who would be good? Then a couple of people whose opinions I value called to suggest that I consider doing it. My wife and I talked about it, prayed about it, felt led to do it, and so we did. It's worked out very well.

Howell's parents were New Deal Democrats. His own political philosophy slowly evolved from that early shared sensibility with his parents until, finally, he became a Reagan Republican.

The man I desperately wanted to engage on behalf of the *Brown* Scholarships was someone who, though strong in the conservative principles of government he had come to embrace, still brought an uncommon depth of nuance, a deeper understanding of both sides of the political aisle than perhaps might those who had been dyed-in-the-wool conservatives or liberals their whole lives.

THE FIRST SESSION OF the Virginia House of Burgesses convened at Jamestown on July 30, 1619. The first slave ships arrived at the settlement before the end of the following month. Representative government for white males and enslavement of African Americans became institutions on the shores of a so-called New World almost simultaneously, beginning a tortuous and shared journey, a separate and unequal odyssey down a long and wounding road.

Three centuries, eight decades, and five years after that historic summer at Jamestown—historic for opposite reasons—the successor to the House of Burgesses had a chance to reach out to the descendants of slaves and say: "I am sorry for massive resistance and this is what I intend to do about it."

On March 22, 2004, the speaker of the House of Delegates, William J. Howell, told me he thought the Virginia General Assembly would do precisely that if Warner sent legislators his promised budget amendment for veto day.

"Yes, massive resistance was a dreadful spot on Virginia history," Howell said, after I'd shared John Hurt's story with him. Howell quietly declared that full funding for the *Brown* Scholarships would happen when the governor sent down an amendment.

This year. Budget crisis or no budget crisis.

With his words, I found myself in the calm eye of the legislative storm. No thunder. No lightning. No swirling rush of wind making it hard to stand upright, much less move forward. Momentary peace, instead.

So much relentless struggle had been necessary to reach these simple words that nobody else would speak. And the man who was speaking them had the political power to make those words come true in the House of Delegates, a governing body so far adamantly opposed to any state funding for the *Brown* Scholarships.

Trying to contain my joy, I told Howell that I was glad to hear him say that because I was concerned that, with the entire nation watching, partisan politics would doom the governor's scholarship budget amendment.

Howell responded with vigor. "That's just not true," he said, telling me I "should not think like that."

The speaker again said he believed a Warner budget amendment would pass on veto day. "It's going to be OK. I can't imagine it would be defeated." Howell added, though, "I've been wrong before." Then he said, "I'll talk it up and see what we can do."

I told Howell that I knew some people asked why these individuals didn't finish school after the five years of massive resistance. I recalled standing next to a senator, waiting for the elevator in the General Assembly building some weeks earlier. "My parents would have kicked my butt if I hadn't gone back to school," he told me as we discussed the *Brown* Scholarship legislation. And that senator was one of our supporters. In fact, he was my Senate patron, Benjamin Lambert, an African American. Lambert had surely confronted racism and discrimination during his lifetime but he did not confront massive resistance in his own childhood. He had not walked even one yard in John Hurt's shoes.

I told Howell that those asking that question don't understand the "massive" in massive resistance. These human beings in Prince Edward County "were slammed." There was an emotional and psychological impact that someone who did not experience the trauma of massive resistance could not possibly comprehend.

When I hung up the phone, I knew the political storm against full funding for the *Brown* Scholarships would rage through the rest of the regular session of the General Assembly. But the eye of that storm had foreshadowed its own demise on veto day. Sixty days after the regular session ended, opposition would blow itself out. It just had to.

Speaker Howell would later tell me, "I don't think you'll have any problem. I'd be flabbergasted [if it didn't pass]."

The speaker of the House of Delegates is not given to hyperbole. "Flabbergasted' was a big deal: "flabbergasted" was not winning by a nose.

"Flabbergasted" became my word of the day.

What a curious set of contradictory circumstances it all was.

Meaningful funding for the *Brown S* scholarships looked impossible to win during the regular session. At the moment, with the House of Delegates' GOP majority opposed to any state funding at all, we were hanging onto the Senate's proposal of $100,000 over two years, wondering what might happen in conference committee.

At the same time, I'd just been assured that if the governor did send down a $2 million budget amendment on veto day it would pass. This just shows how the dynamic changes on veto day, with the added focus on a handful of items to be decided on a closely observed roll call vote. The "raw politics" of it, according to Speaker Howell, simply would not allow a vote against Warner's budget amendment. There was no political cover on veto day.

That was exactly what I had been counting on.

As I shared the glad tidings with John Stokes, I told him that the April 21 rally was now even more important. Regardless of where the General Assembly was on its budget schedule, I said, the rally would answer the question on everyone's mind: Will people use the scholarships? That would reinforce passage of the governor's amendment whenever veto day did occur (the budget fight had extended the regular session and veto day had been pushed back accordingly).

Stokes was electric. "That would be the balm, water in the well," he told me, the joy in his voice splashing like a cloudburst in the desert. "So often my people have gone to the well and there was no water."

Where we were headed now, Stokes said, "The people would be bathed in healing balm."

And, of course, I called John Hurt. The speaker of the House of Delegates says the scholarship funding will pass on veto day, I told him. There had been so many prayers lifted up from Prince Edward County for so many years, I said, and this is the Holy Spirit at work answering them.

And you at work, Hurt told me. "You have been called and raised up" to do this, he said, bringing me once again to my knees. "This is your purpose in life."

Be faithful to a cause as if it *were* your purpose, your destiny in life, I came to understand, and it can become just that.

Since February 18, 2003, I had simply tried to be as strong for the *Brown* Scholarships—and for those who would use them—as I could.

But, the *Brown* Scholarships were clearly a destiny shared, one that now included the speaker of the House of Delegates.

10

Bound for Civil Rights History

The five yellow school buses heading east on U.S. Route 460 from Prince Edward County on the morning of April 21, 2004, appeared to be no different than any other school bus on any other road in the Commonwealth of Virginia. But anyone looking closely through the windows would have seen no children's faces.

The Prince Edward County Public School buses were filled instead with men and women who as children had been turned away from the county's public schools by massive resistance. Now, county school buses were driving them to the State Capitol. They were on a mission to give Doubting Thomases in the House of Delegates and Senate a chance to see and feel the community's determination to use fully funded *Brown* Scholarships.

Bits and pieces of conversation skimmed above the sound of the engine, but my attention was focused on the man sitting beside me. John Hurt and I were two grown men believing in Barbara Rose Johns's "we would live happily ever after" dream.

Both of us were scheduled to speak during the rally, which would include the governor. Warner had quickly accepted the invitation. Moreover, Qualls had called me at home, asking if I'd like the governor to ceremonially sign—right there on the Capitol steps—Senator Lambert's bill creating the scholarship program. It was a wonderful offer by the governor. With these men and women watching, that moment would add power and meaning.

Governor Warner had officially signed SB 230 into law on April 16. With Baskerville's House bill dead and buried, the Senate bill was our lifeline. The *Brown v. Board of Education* Scholarship Program and Fund had been established. So far without any money, of course—the Senate's $100,000 was a proposal to be threshed out with House conferees—but the scholarship program would be fully funded if Warner's budget amendment triumphed on veto day.

I was glad to see Warner wasn't keeping quiet about what he'd just done with his pen. He issued a statement, "I have previously announced my support for this bill and I am proud to have signed it into law. Additionally, I will work to provide adequate state funding in our budget review process."

In their coverage of the signing, both the *Washington Post* and the *Richmond Times-Dispatch* highlighted the promise of a $2 million budget amendment. I knew the House Speaker believed that state funding would pass both houses of the General Assembly in the veto session.

As THE BUSES CARRIED us toward Richmond, Hurt looked at me and repeated the sentiment he had expressed in our phone conversation a few weeks earlier. His words rolled over me like the reverberating rumble of winter thunder. "This is definitely," he said, "your purpose in life." Through the years, similar words would be spoken to me by others within the black community. The words, and those who spoke them, never failed to lay hands upon me and give me strength. I replied to Hurt—who dreamed of becoming a preacher some day—that God being with us was the only way we've gotten this far. But he believed that already.

When we arrived at the Capitol, we gathered across the street outside the General Assembly building. Wearing large purple political campaign buttons that declared "Massive Redemption," we wanted to make it impossible for any delegate or senator to miss our message. The state budget battle between the House and Senate had sent the General Assembly deep into extra innings. April 21 was no longer veto day, but our presence was if anything even more significant—its meaning would have time to resonate with the legislators.

The hundred or so of us then walked toward the Capitol, passing the statue of the late Harry Flood Byrd Sr. The children Byrd's Machine had locked out of school walked on. Byrd's eyes stared blindly ahead. There could

John Hurt had completed the first grade when Prince Edward County's Board of Supervisors voted in June 1959 to shut down public education. On the morning of April 21, 2004, Hurt boarded a school bus for the journey to the Virginia state Capitol where he spoke on behalf of state funding for the **Brown v. Board of Education Scholarship Program and Fund.** *(Photo by Lacy B. Ward Sr.)*

be no further pursuit of John Hurt as he stepped up to the microphone on the steps of the state Capitol, which had been designed by Thomas Jefferson, author of "all men are created equal."

"All my life's been a struggle without education. I made it by the grace of God," Hurt said, the words strong and clear, ringing through the microphone on the lectern, Warner standing just to his left.

"I stand here today as a fifty-four-year-old student that will be the first one to be on the bus if this bill [is funded] . . . The decision you make today, you have to live with. The wrong one was made, but today you have the chance to make the right one." The morning sun and breeze played lightly with leaves that were a color of green that only spring can bring.

"Growing up in Prince Edward County, as I look back over my life, it's hard for me to stand here without crying . . . The applications I never could fill out for a job. Nobody knows what I went through," he said. John

Stokes, Senator Marsh and Delegate Baskerville were also standing by his side. "When I walked into a supermarket when they had a contest there where you fill out the entry form, I couldn't do it. The education I got today, I got it after I was grown and had two kids."

No victim here. Not John Hurt. A casualty, yes, but one who had looked life in the eye and then gone out and lived it, despite the school closings. Hurt's words and the key points of all who spoke during the rally were published in a front-page story in the *Farmville Herald*.

"The embarrassment I had to go through," he said, dressed in a gray suit, speaking at a lectern bearing the seal of the Commonwealth of Virginia. "Can you imagine being a great big boy sitting in school with somebody that's just starting out in school on the first day and they are a lot smarter than you? They're making fun of you. Kids can be real mean. It just got to the point that I would rather take a beating, or anything, than return to school. But today, I would return to school and would smile and be giving God the glory."

Hurt was followed by Dorothy Holcomb. "In 1959, I remember being a happy nine-year-old finishing up fourth grade with the anticipation of a fun summer and returning to school in the fall," she said. "Never in my wildest dreams could I have imagined that I would never attend public schools in Prince Edward County again, but this is what happened to me and my life changed forever. I remember sitting on the steps of my home fully devastated and I was not alone in sharing those emotions. Many of us experienced the catastrophic reality of what all this meant."

Holcomb was among the few children of Prince Edward County able to go to school in an adjacent county. After two years of no formal education, she attended school in Appomattox, where her father worked. When the third year of massive resistance approached, her father rented a house just over the Prince Edward County line. As Holcomb recounts in her book, *Educated in Spite of . . . A Promise Kept,* he drove his children to that empty house in Appomattox every morning on his way to work. Holcomb and her brother and sister waited behind the building, running out when they heard the approaching school bus, a real-life stage play with genuine props to make it seem that the family lived there. A new mailbox had even been erected. Eventually, the Holcomb family actually did move to Appomattox.

In addition to the "reality and pain of separation from friends and family and the comfort of your neighborhood," she said, the family "experienced extreme financial hardship in what it meant to have to commute and have to relocate from your county and attempt to get an education."

Speaking for her generation, Holcomb said, "we realized the plague of illiteracy, poverty, and joblessness caused by a lack of education. We realized the embarrassment of returning to school after five years without an education and being a twenty-two- or twenty-three-year-old senior or going to school for the first time as a nine-year-old.

"I know this seems like fiction," Holcomb assured those listening, "but it's true."

While waiting to board the bus to Richmond that morning, Holcomb had seen a fourth-grade classmate she had happily wished to "have a good summer" at the end of the 1959 school year. Both were looking forward to fifth grade in the fall and another happy chapter in life's journey.

Holcomb's friend was aware that in 2003 the General Assembly had formally expressed its "profound regret" for the 1959 closing of schools in Prince Edward County and more generally for the state's role in massive resistance to desegregation. Now, decades later, preparing to board a school bus with Holcomb once again, the friend had told her, "You can give me all the regrets you want. But what I regret most is that I did not get the opportunity to get my education."

"She said," Holcomb continued, telling the story as her friend listened, "'I wanted to be a nurse.' She said, 'I'm 53 years old and I still want to be a nurse.' This is why we're here today . . . You legislators have the power today to give my fourth-grade classmate what she so desperately wants and, even more, what she deserves."

When a hurricane devastates a community, she continued "the government is quick to appropriate funds to rescue the victims and rebuild the damage. But a wave of ignorance comes through an entire community and deprives innocent children of their constitutional right to a public education and nothing is done. In 1959, the children did not deserve to be locked out of their schools and be deprived of an education. It's time to give them what they deserve now. Today."

How COULD ANY DOUBTING Thomas resist recanting disbelief?

Senator Marsh hammered the point home. "When this bill was legislated in the Senate and when it was debated, we were told that it couldn't be funded because we don't believe there were people who were hurt by the school closing and we don't believe there are people who would take advantage of any educational opportunity if we passed the bill and funded the bill. But look behind me and you can see," Marsh declared.

When the amens and applause subsided, he continued, "Justice works in a strange way. The bill that came out of the Senate was sort of emasculated and we didn't have the funding. Because of the way our system works—the system of checks and balances—we've given a lot of power to our governor and he has the will and the ability to breathe life into this bill . . ."

Noting that most of those gathered on the Capitol steps probably had voted for Warner, Marsh said, "so it is fitting and appropriate that he comes to the rescue and resolves this in a way that Virginia will not have to hang its head in shame . . . This is a happy moment in the life of Virginia. And I'm so pleased that when the issue came to the governor he had the wisdom and the courage and the foresight to say, 'I'm not going to disappoint these people anymore. I'm not going to let them be hurt anymore.'"

I stepped behind the lectern shortly after 11 a.m. Governor Warner was just to my left. I had a copy of my speech but those words were not as important as what I was going to do with the words on a single sheet of paper in my other hand. Those words had been signed by 4,500 white adult citizens of Prince Edward County in 1956 and presented to the Board of Supervisors. When my speech was over, I held up high for all to see the copy of the white community's petition to shut down public education entirely rather than integrate schools. I announced what it was. Then I placed it against the microphone. I wanted the sound of what happened next to speak loud and clear.

We, the undersigned citizens of Prince Edward County, Virginia,

The author speaking during the April 21, 2004, rally on the steps of the Virginia Capitol on behalf of state funding for the Brown v. Board of Education *Scholarship Program and Fund. To the author's immediate left are Delegate Viola Baskerville, Governor Mark R. Warner, and John Stokes. (Photo by Lacy B. Ward Sr.)*

hereby affirm our conviction that the separation of the races in the public schools of this County is absolutely necessary, and do affirm that we prefer to abandon public schools and educate our children in some other way if that be necessary to preserve separation of the races in the schools of this county.

We pledge our support of the Board of Supervisors of Prince Edward County in their firm maintenance of this policy.

Then I slowly ripped those words apart, balled up the two halves, and threw them to the ground.

"This is a new day," I said, "and Governor Warner and the General Assembly have a new covenant with the people."

The balled-up copy of the petition tumbled down the Capitol steps. Charlie Taylor, who in 1959 had been looking forward to his senior year, grabbed it—"I didn't want you to be arrested for littering," he told me afterward, in all seriousness. I learned later that he kept both pieces of the torn words, that had torn a community apart, as a keepsake of that 2004 moment when we put ourselves back together again: a moment that included Governor Mark Warner placing a huge exclamation mark on the rally by ceremoniously signing Senator Lambert's bill.

"I do know that fifty years out from *Brown*, forty years after the end of massive resistance," Warner said, "we can do something here in Virginia to try to right that wrong. And we can make sure to future Virginians that we're sending a message that says, 'This kind of action will never again happen in Virginia. Because of the brave people that went before you, some of us now will have the responsibility to do the right thing.'"

THE WAY HAD NOT always been smooth, but eleven months after saying "I'll fight with you on this," here he was, standing with us on the steps of the Capitol, keeping his word. The impact of the physical presence of the governor by our side was immense. I had seen it on the faces of those waiting with me when Warner walked around the corner and climbed the steps to join us. My own spirits had lifted. Press releases are important. They spread the word. But when someone who is counted on as much as I had been depending on Governor Warner actually stands publicly at one's side, the commitment becomes concrete for all to see. His presence sent a message to us and to the General Assembly.

"There's lots of reasons why we need a budget," Warner continued, "but one of the reasons we need a budget is so that I can submit a budget amendment to make sure that we fund this *Brown v. Board of Education* . . . massive resistance scholarship."

Those were trumpeting words. Coupled with Speaker Howell's "it's going to happen that way," Jericho's walls were trembling.

I approached the governor after his remarks had concluded the rally, just before the bill signing. "It's a good day for Virginia, a good day for the nation," I told him.

He stopped for a moment. "Yes," he said. "A good day for Virginia and the nation." He then turned toward the people who had stood behind us. Their faces were lit with joy. They had stood next to a governor of the Commonwealth of Virginia who was standing with them. A governor who had promised the balm would come to Gilead. I was elated. We all were.

With that, and with *Today* show cameras rolling, Warner sat behind the wooden table beside the lectern and signed his name. When the cheers died down, he smiled and asked, "Who wants the pen?"

A pen as mighty as a plowshare—if we got the $2 million on veto day.

Riding back to Farmville, what I noticed most was the happiness that radiated from so many faces and the sounds of their voices.

During a phone conversation the next day, John Stokes told me, "It's a new world."

Five days after I ripped up the copy of the massive resistance petition on the Capitol steps, Steve Wall pulled me aside. He told me that his father, William B. Wall, had been angered by my action. Steve said his father had pointed out that five thousand people in the community had signed the petition and might not agree with my tearing it up.

I steeled myself for another confrontation with Bill. But he never said a thing to me about what I had done. Nor did I hear a single word of criticism from anyone in the community.

Stokes was right. A nascent world was beckoning.

Just how new it could become would be made clear to me by civil rights legend Julian Bond less than three weeks later.

Bond helped found the Student Nonviolent Coordinating Committee (SNCC) while a student at Morehouse College and served as the organization's communications director. SNCC played a crucial role in the civil rights movement during the 1960s. Bond was later elected to the Georgia House of Representatives and then to the Georgia Senate. Bond was also the first president of the Southern Poverty Law Center. On May 8, 2004, he was national chairman of the NAACP and the commencement speaker at Longwood University. I wanted his ear, if for a single minute. I got an hour when the university seated me next to Bond at the post-commencement lunch. The time was not wasted.

"I'll gin it up," Bond said, promising his support at a crucial stage of the journey. What you're attempting to do, he pointed out, has never been done before. If you are successful, Bond stressed, the *Brown* Scholarships would become "the first civil rights-era reparation" in the nation.

Without knowing it, we were attempting to make civil rights history.

As expected, Governor Warner's veto day budget amendment would be our only chance of doing so. Two weeks after our rally, the conference committee's resolution of the differences in the House and Senate budget proposals made certain of that.

The budget conferees were brutal to the *Brown* Scholarships. The nine conferees—five from the House and four from the Senate—cut the Senate's funding in half. In a state budget of more than $59 billion for the 2004–06 biennium, we learned on May 6 that they had included only $50,000—$25,000 per year.

Two days later, the General Assembly approved the conferees' deal, adopting the budget and avoiding a state government shutdown.

Had it not been for Warner's promise of the veto day budget amendment and House Speaker Howell's belief that it would pass, the bread-crumb funding would have devastated me. But Senator Lambert's bill, with its small sum of money, had made it to the governor's desk. Now he could act.

The reconvened veto day session, originally set for April 21, would be June 16. Victory or defeat would be declared on that day.

11

The Promised Land

The phone call from Ellen Qualls made me feel like I'd awakened in a room where all of the furniture had been rearranged. Or in another house altogether. I opened my eyes to a miracle on May 26. Manna from heaven. One million pieces of scholarship funding manna.

None of us had known—not the governor, not the speaker, nor any member of the Virginia General Assembly—but someone had been watching silently and from afar as the General Assembly moved toward adjournment of its 2004 regular session.

One of the richest men in the world had been following—thanks to the media coverage generated by the governors' February 13 joint statement—the *Brown* Scholarship crusade's tortuous progress through the state legislature. Out of the blue, John Kluge promised to donate $1 million for the *Brown v. Board of Education* Scholarship Program and Fund.

Kluge, a German-born philanthropist and billionaire who lived in Charlottesville, contacted U.S. Senator John Warner to make his $1 million offer. The senator then contacted Governor Warner. The rest would become a part of civil rights reparations history.

Qualls told me that Governor Warner's budget amendment was now changing and would work like this: Warner will still send down a $2 million budget amendment on veto day, with $1 million of it state funds and $1 million being Kluge's donation. She said the message to legislators would be, "You voted down $2 million once and now you have a second chance and we can get $1 million free."

In a press release, Governor Warner called Kluge's gift an "extraordinarily generous offer that gives" Virginia another chance to provide educational opportunity to those who had been denied their schooling, and perhaps to "send a message of reconciliation and healing."

The governor continued, "Accordingly, I will submit a budget amendment to the legislature that matches this donation at the level of $1 million, and also appropriates Mr. Kluge's donation for a total of $2 million. It is my hope that legislators will accept this amendment, and I am so grateful to Mr. Kluge for making the offer.'"

Qualls told me that neither the governor nor his administration had anything to do with the Kluge donation, which came through Senator Warner and was being presented to the legislature, with Kluge's blessing, as a challenge matching grant.

Kluge remained off stage throughout. He never issued a statement and was never quoted. I mailed a letter of thanks to the chairman of Metromedia via his office in New York City.

I MOVED ACROSS THE sloping meadow toward the woods awaiting me on either side of the Appomattox River in the green-gold of early evening. Veto day was less than forty-eight hours away. I'd received a phone call from a Columbus, Ohio, firefighter, an African American who had been raised in Prince Edward County. During a forty-minute conversation, he spoke about the *Brown* Scholarship crusade and said, "I won't look at it as a glass that is half full. I am happy with it. Elated. I'm just pissed off it took a reporter in Farmville to tell them in Virginia they needed to do this." No, I thought, perhaps the editor of the *Farmville Herald* was precisely the person who needed to do so, given the newspaper's editorial insistence that schools be closed in opposition to the *Brown* decision.

I walked toward a forest trail at Appomattox Courthouse National Historical Park. Some of my ancestors had worn blue during the Civil War. Others had worn gray. I'd seen a photograph of one of them at my grandparents' house. About a mile away, Confederate General Robert E. Lee and Union General Ulysses S. Grant had concluded the war my relatives fought against each other. There was no rifle in my hand, just a simple walking stick, as I crossed the small footbridge over the river.

"You are a blessing from the Lord for a big group of people and you should feel joy," the man on the phone had told me. ". . . There is just a big group of people who are very thankful."

Talking to someone "who has made a difference in this," he added, had given him the motivation to work through "my own issues and my own pain from those days. You'll be in my prayers . . . It's a Band-Aid, but much better than nothing and it gives me some sort of peace."

The gentleman told me he was thinking about "just how different it could have been for individuals and the community if people had not been split apart. The depth of this is so huge . . . I thank God I have seen this come about in my lifetime."

I thanked God for that, too.

John Hurt, Rita Moseley, Dorothy Holcomb, John Stokes, and I were among the dozens sitting in the visitor's gallery above the House floor as the minutes ticked down toward gavel time on June 16. We were there to witness creation of the first civil rights-era reparation in U.S. history. Governor Warner's budget amendment was agenda item No. 10.

I caught Speaker Howell's eye and waved from the gallery. During one of our phone conversations he'd told me I needed to relax. "I know this is your baby and you've invested a lot of your soul in this," he'd said, "but I think you're going to be okay." Subsequently, a June 4 *Richmond Times-Dispatch* story by Pamela Stallsmith, reported: "A spokesman for Howell said the Speaker plans to support the [budget] amendment." I knew Howell was going to vote for the budget amendment but I regarded those words as a sonic boom in terms of their potential impact on GOP House members.

Howell's friendly wave in return offered reassurance, but, of course, then came a nerve-wracking delay. At noon, the House went into immediate recess, both parties caucusing, until 1 p.m.

As an Independent, Delegate Abbitt—a former Democrat who left the party to keep the GOP from running a candidate against him—did not caucus with either party. Our political wingman during two critical committee meetings was waiting on the floor of the House. Noticing me in the gallery, Abbitt got up, walked over and said, in a voice meant for my ears only, "You're going to have somebody speak against it": Delegate R. Lee Ware, a Republican from Powhatan.

That news collided with my confidence. Did Ware represent a group of delegates who might rise in opposition, or was he speaking only for himself? Much would hinge on the answer to that question. A full-fledged debate, I feared, could derail everything. My heart began to race and my mouth became dry as desert air.

When the party caucusing was over, I got Delegate Hogan's attention. "Is everything OK?" I asked from my gallery seat just above him. Hogan seemed to grimace but said, "I think we're going to be OK."

That lukewarm response made me wonder how strong any dissent might be. I was worried about the House but also concerned about any negative influence it might have on the Senate, because I saw the two most powerful Republican senators, Finance Committee Chairman John Chichester and Majority Leader Walter Stosch, sitting along the wall of the House chamber, ready to take in every word. The Senate had adjusted its veto day schedule. The House was going to act first.

Stosch's aide had made it clear the day before that the senator was going to "listen and learn" from the debate because he had not made up his mind. What happened in the House, I felt, would influence deliberations in the Senate. One way or another, it seemed clear, the fate of the *Brown* Scholarships would be decided right here. Victory in the House would lead to triumph in the Senate.

WHEN LEADING THE FINAL laps, race car drivers worry about every little thing they hear or feel in the engine, suspension, or transmission. The tiniest bump makes some drivers fear disaster will strike before they cross the finish line. I could relate.

The first "bump" on the way to the finish line came when, as Abbitt had warned, Delegate Ware—using the one-objection rule—opened the discussion, which I fully reported in the *Farmville Herald*. The one-objection rule allows any of the House's one hundred members to select a legislative item so that it can be debated on the floor. Ware opposed the budget amendment.

The law in civil matters, he said, requires a demonstration that damage has been done.

The House, Ware noted, had previously expressed in its 2003 resolution its regret for the closing of schools and "beyond regret it is not possible for us to go . . . It is impossible for us to understand or condemn what people did in the past."

Nor, he argued, was it possible for the legislature to "compensate" for the past. Could "a decision by the General Assembly restore us to Eden" by making the descendants of Cain compensate the descendants of Abel? "All history is fraught with strife" and legislators "must rise above the past" and not attempt to judge it or redeem it. Political correctness "has stifled us . . . There are many sides to this, countless sides, and we can't judge who's right or wrong. . . ."

At that moment, I fully understood the phrase "my heart was in my throat." When Ware sat down, I was terribly anxious about which voice and what words would be spoken next.

Saying that he agreed with Ware on the issue of reparations, Delegate Clifford L. Athey Jr., a Front Royal Republican, nevertheless defended Warner's budget amendment: "We aren't reaching back to the slave trade . . . These people are still here." Noting that blacks and whites had been harmed when schools were closed in Warren County, part of his House district, Athey said approving the scholarship funding was important "to the legacy of Virginia and how we move into the future."

Delegate Ken Melvin, a Portsmouth Democrat respected by House Republicans, noted that "some of those" harmed by massive resistance, who would be eligible for the scholarships, "are above us"—in fact the House gallery was full of them.

Melvin declared that despite the fact that there was no one he respected more than Ware, "I vehemently disagree with him on this." He traced the history of massive resistance in the state and noted the role played by a Virginia governor and the General Assembly, adding, "We can't undo history but we can tell how we feel about it and do something about it."

Another Republican legislator stressed that the casualties of massive resistance had been "directly affected by an act of the Virginia General Assembly and an act can be undone by a subsequent legislature. We can never undo the past but this is a small attempt to rectify the actions of the past."

The original appropriation of $50,000 was not enough, he continued. "Will $1 million be enough? I think this is fair, as fair as we can be now."

As the supportive voices continued to speak, I began to realize that the first bump on the way to the finish line today might be the only one.

DURING HIS COMMENTS AGAINST the budget amendment, Ware had noted groups of people such as the Huguenots and Jews who had been persecuted throughout history. A delegate then asked Ware if the Virginia Constitution had been amended in 1870 to make free public education a constitutional right. Ware responded that it had been, yes.

Did the Virginia Constitution, the delegate then asked, give special rights, privileges, and protections to any of the persecuted peoples Delegate Ware had cited?

The answer, of course, was no. Virginia was responsible for its own history, not Europe's, and on this day Virginia could do something to atone for its massive resistance.

Democratic Delegate Albert C. Eisenberg of Arlington responded emphatically to Ware's remarks: "I believe you *can* look back . . . We can look back and say it was wrong and we can make amends . . . What happened affected a whole generation in Virginia and the United States and hate was the sensibility in vogue." He said that what was done "hurts, not just one group, it hurts us all and we can say it was wrong. And doing so would be a good thing, not just for the past but also for the future."

All during the debate, Baskerville remained silent and in her seat. Wisely, in my opinion, she had decided not to make herself a diversionary target for Republican antipathy.

Besides, after House Majority Leader Morgan Griffith spoke in support of the budget amendment there really was no need for anyone else to say anything. Griffith stressed the point I had been making with Republicans—the GOP minority in the General Assembly attempted to block massive resistance in the 1950s. That piece of strategy was paying off. Griffith asked Melvin if it was true that seven Republicans had tried to stop massive resistance and that the closing of schools to prevent their integration was a Democratic initiative.

Melvin said that was "historically accurate."

Enough words had been spoken. Only Ware had objected to the budget amendment. All other comments, from Republicans and Democrats, had been in support of Warner's budget amendment.

With Senators Chichester and Stosch still in attendance, the vote was taken. As the totals glowed on the electronic voting board, it was clear that the Speaker of the House was not going to be flabbergasted.

The final tally was astonishing: ninety-four yeas, including Speaker Howell, and just four nays, with two delegates not voting. We had won, 94–4.

A joyous roar rose from the gallery. Despite that transgression of gallery protocol, Speaker Howell did not so much as raise his gavel an inch. In fact, I saw a quick smile cross his face as he looked up at the gallery. He and I made eye contact, each waving as we had prior to the session.

I embraced John Hurt and Dorothy Holcomb. Our dream had just come true.

There were thirty-three amendments left on the agenda but none of us cared. We could not sit still. If the House was to continue its business, we had to take our rejoicing out into the hallway where we could talk, shout, hug, and wipe tears from our eyes.

Our faces and voices told the story. Nobody who missed the vote needed to ask the outcome. Rita Moseley and I had raced ahead of a snowstorm to testify before the House Education Committee in January. Winter had gone, spring had come, and in five days it would be the summer solstice, the day of most light. The journey had been long and it had been difficult.

Soon, most began to make their way out of the Capitol. I bid them farewell. The months-long not-winnable House funding vote had been won. The Senate vote, however, had not been taken. Despite being certain of victory there, I was going nowhere.

The Senate vote was almost anticlimactic, and anticlimax never felt so good. As the session began, Senator Lambert looked up at me, smiled and raised his index finger in what I read as a $1 million signal. Amendment No. 10, fully funding the scholarships, was grouped as part of a block of amendments on which the Senate expected no problems. Senator Chichester made the motion to approve the block and his fellow senators did so, 36–0.

Lieutenant Governor Tim Kaine, a supporter from the beginning, congratulated me from the Senate floor, looking up with a huge smile on his face. Kaine's father-in-law, former Governor Linwood Holton, had been instrumental, along with former governors Charles Robb and Gerald Baliles, in persuading Governor Mark Warner to issue the joint statement supporting the *Brown* Scholarships with adequate funding.

The Senate and the House finally adjourned their 115-day longest ever General Assembly session. The tax-and-spend debate had sent legislators into an unprecedented overtime beyond the scheduled sixty-day run.

After sixteen long months of continuous mental, emotional, and physical effort, there was nothing more I had to do to win funding for the *Brown v. Board of Education* Scholarships. As I lay that burden down, I felt an aching begin to spread through my body and I experienced a feeling of utter exhaustion. I was worn and crumpled, walking on air but heavy as lead. I wanted to sing, to shout, to laugh and cry—or just be very still and very quiet for a very long time.

John Stokes and I ran into Speaker Howell in a Capitol hallway. The speaker and I smiled, shared the handshake we'd both looked forward to, and I acknowledged, "Yes, you told me not to worry."

Stokes thanked Howell for his support but the speaker pointed to me and said, "He did all the work."

The truth is that we all did what we could. None of our work individually would have come to much without all of our collective work. As Julian Bond had predicted, we had literally made history. We had done so for human beings who truly deserved every step we had taken.

Heading toward my car, I intersected the path of Senator Chichester as he was walking away from the Capitol, his treacherous budget crisis-solving work done. For months, I had been frustrated and angered by his position on scholarship funding. I could have walked on past. We had never met and he would not have recognized me. But the man had come through this day. I introduced myself, sincerely thanked him for his support and shook his hand. Then both of us walked on. Once again, the nearby statue of Harry F. Byrd Sr., the author of massive resistance, could do nothing.

ALONG U.S. 460 FIFTEEN miles from my home, blue sky began to appear through the clouds of a departing thunder storm. I was thinking of John Hurt and what the *Brown* Scholarships might mean to him. I was thinking about how Hurt's seven-year-old world had crumbled in 1959, sending him off to work on a dairy farm instead of going into second grade. I was thinking about how Hurt had never been able to recover what his life might have been without the five years of massive resistance.

My thoughts were on Hurt when I noticed something in the rear view mirror that I'd never seen before while driving. The sunlight shining through the spray from the car's rear tires was making a small rainbow just behind and above the trunk. There was a simple scientific explanation, of course, but it looked the way I felt inside.

12

We Gathered Our Light

For anyone just tuning in to the *Brown* Scholarship crusade, the overwhelming victory would have seemed the simple, straightforward fact that it really should have been in the first place.

A 94–4 triumph in the House? Of course.

A 36 to nil vote in the Senate? Most certainly.

A final overall tally of 130–4? Indubitably.

How could it have turned out any other way?

Anyone just tuning in probably would not believe the answer to that question.

And there was one more question looking for an answer.

Winning this appropriation had been terribly hard—obtaining a simple joint gubernatorial statement in support of the scholarship funding was astonishingly difficult.

Why, then, had it been so easy for Prince Edward County to close down an entire public school system for five years?

THE DAY AFTER THE *Brown* Scholarship's passage through the General Assembly I wrote Governor Warner:

> Thank you for the things you did to help make this possible for our state. I know we had some rough moments but please believe that everything I did was necessary to accomplish this goal. The joint statement of the governors was critical, as was you seeking full funding. I have kept a

diary since last year and it's hard to believe all the things that happened, all the work that needed to be done, and the ways manna always seemed to fall into the wilderness at just the right moment.

God wanted this done. So many prayers had come up from Prince Edward over the last 40 years and now, in this way, they have been answered.

Ultimately, what matters most, of course, is that we did accomplish this mission and Virginia made history in a way that sets an example for the nation and, ultimately, mankind . . . We can be proud of the things we did together to make this happen.

Press secretary Ellen Qualls was among those who had earned my eternal gratitude. I emailed my thanks for her help—"the bottom line is that we accomplished something very good." She replied that she was moved by the final votes. "All bumps in the road aside, you did real good, my friend."

EIGHT DAYS AFTER OUR victory, I saw Governor Warner at the American Legion Auxiliary's Girls State, held every summer at Longwood University, a block from my office. The appearance of the incumbent governor is always the highlight of the week-long civics and leadership session for high school juniors.

After his talk, we had a short visit. There were several Virginia State Troopers and one or two other people nearby, but this was essentially a private moment.

I opened the conversation by again thanking him for making the *Brown* Scholarships a reality. Warner responded by speaking of my "heart" and saying, "You were just, you wouldn't let up . . ." He shook his head slightly and there was a note of wonder in his voice.

It was as genuinely human a moment as anyone could have with a state governor. Warner, the man, the human being, was standing inches from me, his arms spread—his body language amplifying how open and honest he was being—as he searched for the words he wanted to say, a Girls State T-shirt neatly rolled up in his left hand.

When I had first brought the idea to him, Warner continued, he'd had some questions and fear that the legislation would be defeated. He said that he was "never sure it would go through, you know. God bless you."

Thank you, I told him, "for standing with us."

"Hey, Ken," he replied, "There was never any moral ambiguity about it, it was just . . ."

I told Warner that I always knew where his heart was.

"You are greatly to be complimented," he said, and we shared a firm handshake before he stepped toward the car that would take him back to Richmond.

As I walked back to my office, the late-June heat radiating off the pavement, it felt to me that the governor of Virginia had just apologized for not fighting with us sooner and more vigorously. It was an extraordinary moment. Not many politicians would have been so open. It took character to drop the gubernatorial mask and show such vulnerability to the mere editor of a small-town twice-weekly newspaper.

I shared some of those thoughts in an email to Qualls. I knew there was never any moral ambiguity, which is why, I explained, I had pushed him so hard. I knew what was in the governor's heart. I knew what was in the heart of his administration. "We all share in this victory," I wrote.

A decade after the veto-day triumph, Warner, by then a United States Senator, was Longwood University's commencement speaker. After the ceremony, we sat together in a small alcove down the hall from the university president's office. Warner admitted he had thought the scholarships had "no chance" of passing the General Assembly in 2004, but they did so, he said, "through the sheer force of your personality."

The victory was shared, I told Warner, and would not have occurred without his budget amendment.

During an April 2016 phone conversation—when I asked him to write the foreword to this book—he again spoke of his 2004 doubts about the political viability of the *Brown* Scholarships: "I thought, 'We'll never be able to pull this off.' You had such an audacious idea."

Knowing there were sections in my manuscript that would make him wince, I joked with Warner that as he read it he would need to resist wanting to ship me off to Guantanamo Bay. The senator laughed and said he had many memories himself, adding, "I hope our recollections mesh."

Warner wrote the foreword. I respect him for that. Not every politician would have done so without trying to excise or tone down unflattering passages. Warner—who also sent me a United States flag that had been flown over the U.S. Capitol building during the January 20, 2009, inauguration of Barack Obama—did not ask me to change a single word.

WITHIN EACH OF US is a light for all the world, a carpenter's son taught on a hillside by the Sea of Galilee. Those were startling words spoken to people who, as we often do today, felt powerless to shine even the small shadows away. Jesus told them:

> A town that stands on a hill cannot be hidden. When a lamp is lit, it is not put under the meal-tub but on the lamp-stand, where it gives light to everyone in the house. And you, like the lamp, must shed light among your fellows . . ." (Matthew 5:14–16, *The New English Bible*).

Each of us on the *Brown* Scholarship crusade walked such a light into the world for those wounded by massive resistance in Prince Edward County, but also Charlottesville, Norfolk, and Warren County.

The *Brown v. Board of Education* Scholarship Program and Fund could not be hidden. That mustard seed of light, no more than a lightning bug's worth of illumination as it approached the Prince Edward County line as a newborn idea on February 18, 2003, had survived every attempt to hide or extinguish it beneath a bucket.

Regardless of our faith or lack thereof, whether we went to church, temple, mosque, or wouldn't be caught dead in a place of worship, we had brought this light into the world together.

Veto Day 2004 thus joined two other June 16ths that contributed chapters to a national narrative that began when the first slave ships arrived at Jamestown, Virginia, in 1619.

On June 16, 1858, quoting Jesus, Abraham Lincoln famously said: "A house divided against itself cannot stand." Those immortal words were spoken as he accepted the nomination of the Illinois Republican Party to run for the U.S. Senate seat held by Democrat Stephen A. Douglas.

"I believe this government cannot endure, permanently, half slave and half free. I do not expect the Union to be dissolved—I do not expect the house to fall—but I do expect it will cease to be divided," Lincoln continued. "It will become all one thing or all the other."

Lincoln lost that battle to Douglas but he would win a larger war.

Six years later, on June 16, 1864, General Ulysses S. Grant began his pivotal siege of Petersburg, Virginia. The nine-month campaign led to General Robert E. Lee's flight westward and to his eventual surrender to Grant in Appomattox on April 9, 1865, effectively ending the Civil War.

Then on June 16, 2004, the Virginia General Assembly decided the fate of the *Brown v. Board of Education* Scholarship Program and Fund. In so doing, legislators created the country's first civil rights-era reparation—for the casualties of massive resistance, who were themselves the descendants of those emancipated by the Civil War.

But I knew that the "new skin" spoken of by the prophet Jeremiah could never entirely grow over the wound. Some had died, never knowing that balm had come to Gilead. Others lived out of state and did not meet the in-state residency requirement for the scholarships; that barrier, I feared, would only deepen those persons' pain. Others might feel, for reasons I completely understood, that they were unable to go back to school so late in life.

What, then, could the *Brown v. Board of Education* Scholarship Program and Fund hope to achieve so many years after the school closings? Edward H. Peeples, whose data we had relied upon to estimate the number of blacks and whites left without a formal education in Prince Edward County, wrote a heartfelt congratulatory note to Delegate Viola Baskerville, John Stokes, and me. He directly addressed the question.

Peeples had attended our May 8, 2003, meeting with Governor Warner and had helped craft the legislation with the Division of Legislative Services. The associate professor emeritus of preventive medicine at Virginia Commonwealth University is a life-long civil rights activist and the author of *Scalawag: A White Southerner's Journey through Segregation to Human Rights Activism*. He wrote us:

Now, as you know, there will be naysayers who will contend that these two legislative actions are mere symbolism and mean very little. To them I must say that they are both right and wrong. The Regrets Resolution [of 2003] and the Scholarship Fund are in themselves just symbolic because the remedies we can offer today can never match the magnitude and complexities of the wrongs of the past. But what critics of these efforts may fail to realize is that such symbols make an indelible mark on our history and our culture which will inform all future Virginians that these evils of white supremacy are no longer morally tolerable in the commonwealth and those who continue to indulge in them will and must become objects of shame. Such is the prodigious power of moral symbols."

If that was to be our achievement, then every step in the journey was worth it. But, from what John Hurt, John Stokes, Rita Moseley, and others had said to me, I believed the symbolism could be accompanied by something more tangible and personal in the lives of those who used the scholarships.

Assessing the *Brown* Scholarships a year after their enactment, as individuals began to enroll in the program, the *Washington Post* wrote this in an August 5, 2005, editorial entitled "Repaying Segregation's Debt":

The scholarships, which follow a resolution by the General Assembly two years ago expressing its "profound regret" at the school closings, do not heal the wounds inflicted by what was then known in Virginia as its policy of "massive resistance" to integration . . . Nothing that Virginia can do will fully compensate for that disgraceful episode. Still, the scholarships are an appropriate and admirable act of contrition. As Governor Mark R. Warner said, "This at least goes a partial way to [repay] the debt we owe these folks . . ."

If there is an inspirational note to this story, it belongs to Ken Woodley, the crusading editor of the *Farmville Herald* in Prince Edward County, who almost single-handedly conceived the idea of scholarships, campaigned for it in print and personally urged it on Mr. Warner and hesitant lawmakers.

In 1959, Mr. Woodley's own newspaper led the local chorus of opposition to integration, denouncing it as a communist plot against racial purity and the American way. Now the newspaper, under the same family ownership, has backed Mr. Woodley and the scholarships to the hilt. That is a measure of Virginia's progress, and a credit to it.

There were some moments when, yes, I did feel it was a one-man show, but I was never, ever alone on the journey. There was always someone by my side providing vital support at each crucial bend in the serpentine road, and often at precisely the right moment, and just as often, a remarkable companion. There is a wise African proverb that I understand from my *Brown* Scholarship crusade experience to be absolutely true: "If you want to go fast, go alone. If you want to go far, go together."

Furthermore, if the General Assembly had not been poised to express its profound regret for the school closings and if Prince Edward County High School Latin teacher Linwood Davis hadn't been simultaneously advocating honorary diplomas for the casualties of massive resistance, then the idea for state-funded scholarships as reparation might never have entered my head.

Their light ignited my own. But, yes, how far could all of our light really shine?

I KNOW THE SUMMER of 1959 is forever beyond our reach. We cannot make the school closings go away. The fallout from that June day remains historical fact. Somebody needed to have this scholarship idea and do what was necessary to make it real decades ago, when the affected men and women were in their twenties, not their fifties and sixties; when they had their adult lives and career opportunities ahead of them, rather than largely behind them.

That never happened.

This did.

Healing is the most personal of journeys and it varies from individual to individual. For some wounds, a lifetime can be too short for that journey to reach its peaceful end. My prayer is that some degree of healing was helped along its way by the gathering of our light in 2004. There is nobody I wanted that to be true for more than John Hurt.

The only claim I will ever stake is that we tried.

13

Reparation Within the Sorrow

As of the publication of this book, some two hundred and fifty casualties of Prince Edward County's massive resistance have been served by the *Brown v. Board of Education* Scholarship Program and Fund—virtually the number we had projected back in 2004. The first undergraduate degrees were awarded in May 2007 by Saint Paul's College, in Lawrenceville, Virginia. More degrees were awarded the following spring. Among them was a very familiar face.

"That was a dream come true," Rita Odom-Moseley told me.[*] "And I did it not only for myself but for my mom, who passed years and years ago, because she sacrificed so much to send me away to live with strangers just to get my education." My friend, who had outraced the snowstorm with me in January 2004 to testify before the House Education Committee, had subsequently added her mother's maiden name to her own surname as a tribute. "I wanted to fulfill that dream for not only myself, but also for her."

For decades, that opportunity had been beyond her wildest dreams.

"It never entered my mind. I can't even imagine anybody even thinking of the idea. It never occurred to me that anything would come about such as the *Brown* Scholarships," said Odom-Moseley, who retired after working more than thirty-five years in the Prince Edward County Public School System; she had been the high school principal's secretary.

Odom-Moseley, who followed up her bachelor's degree in business

---

[*]   Her comments here are taken from interviews on August 19, 2015, for this book and for a September 6, 2013, front-page story in the *Farmville Herald*.

administration with a master's degree in executive leadership from Liberty University in Lynchburg, Virginia, has been an inspiration to both young and old. "I've always tried to encourage others and I've had many, many people tell me, who have gone back to school—even younger ones that weren't part of the *Brown* Scholarship program—that I was an inspiration in going back. I can see not only the tremendous effect it had on my life but it affected and changed other people's lives, where they're now in school and they're able to get better jobs and they'll be able to look at things in a different way."

She said that before earning her degrees through the *Brown* Scholarship program, "I could only see the inside of the box. After getting all that education, I finally decided to look outside the box."

"So I gave that to them also," she said of those who followed her example and advice by returning to the classroom.

Odom-Moseley's inspiring ripples were felt within her own family, too. Her son had dropped out of college, but seeing his mother earn her degree motivated him; he also went back to St. Paul's and earned his degree.

In July 2008, billionaire philanthropist John Kluge followed through on his $1 million pledge. His handwritten check arrived by regular U.S. mail, in care of Brenda Edwards at the Division of Legislative Services (DLS), in a hand-addressed envelope. That was very good news, but it meant that for the first four years the scholarships had been funded solely by the General Assembly appropriation, through Warner's budget amendment, for which so many had fought so hard in 2004.

Until her retirement in the spring of 2017, the *Brown* Scholarship Program was overseen by the relentlessly dedicated Edwards, the DLS Senior Research Associate who had helped us craft the idea into legislation in 2003. The program is administered under the direction of a *Brown v. Board of Education* Scholarship Committee whose members are legislators and private citizens appointed by the governor.

The scholarships cover the entire educational spectrum, including approved transitional education programs; the General Education Development Certificate and College Level Examination Program; Adult Basic Education offered by Virginia public schools; comprehensive Virginia community college programs; career and technical education or training at Virginia community colleges; and two- and four-year undergraduate, master's, doctorate, and professional degree programs at accredited Virginia public and private institutions of higher education.

During its 2005 legislative session, the General Assembly passed SB 1034 to correct language deficiencies we knew were contained in 2004's historic SB 230 creating the *Brown v. Board of Education* Scholarship Program and Fund. Also patroned by Senator Lambert, the new bill amended and reorganized the original statute, according to Virginia's Legislative Information Service website. SB 1034 included "several technical amendments to provide clarity and consistency" and reinstated "language inadvertently omitted" in the 2004 legislation. Of greatest importance, SB 1034 allowed the *Brown* Scholarships program to receive Kluge's $1 million donation, as well as "funds from any source." It moved quietly and easily through the legislature.

Virginia's Martin Luther King Jr. Commission, which formally put its official weight behind the *Brown* Scholarship legislation, embraced the designation of Baskerville and Lambert—to whom I had gone on February 18, 2003—as patrons in the House and Senate, respectively. That dual legislative track, it had been hoped, would increase the odds of passage. In the end, that is what happened. One of the two bills died. But that meant the *Brown* Scholarships lived.

The program has allocated the majority of its $2 million. Enough funds remain to complete the educational journeys of those already using the scholarships. The General Assembly's 2004 question over scholarship interest and use has been emphatically answered.

What else could have been stolen from children that they would have wanted so much again in their lives decades later? Education was no bike or toy. It was everything they might have been. And something, somehow, they still became.

But I believe that through their perseverance they had become so much more already. Whether they used a *Brown* Scholarship or not.

ONE OF THOSE WHO remained shut out was John Hurt. Prince Edward County schools closed the summer after Hurt completed first grade. Instead of seeing him take a seat in a second-grade classroom, the fall of 1959 saw the young boy go to work on a dairy farm. What Hurt's life might have been fell to pieces. He had never stopped trying to pick them back up.

But even after the scholarships became available, working days and nights left him no time for classes. A vital part of me was crushed by that news. Yet he had still achieved his dream of pastoring a church, he told me when we spoke on the lakeside patio of the Farmville-Prince Edward Community Library in the fall of 2015.

"Even though I couldn't use the scholarship fund, God made a lot of ways for me that opened a lot of doors," Hurt told me, "and stuff I thought I would never do, God made ways for me to do them."

Hurt was still working for the Virginia Department of Transportation when we spoke. Buffalo Shook, Inc., where he had worked nights, had closed the previous year and the huge facility was torn down after the property was sold to a developer.

"Don't get me wrong, I still struggle with my reading and stuff like that," Hurt said, "but I haven't had a sermon or engagement to do anything that God didn't empower me to do. And this is where I am right now."

There was quiet, humble nobility to this man, in addition to his enduring inner strength and faith. Despite losing his second source of income, Hurt refused to accept pay from his congregation. "I have yet took a penny from the church. They did one time, without me knowing it, give me a $250 check but I have yet to be paid for pastoring, and this is my motto: The Bible says 'Freely you have received, now freely give.'"

Hurt's reaction to seeing so many others using the scholarships confirmed my every impression of him. "Sometimes you feel like you're forgotten," Hurt revealed, adding that, "when I found out that the scholarships wouldn't do me any good the scripture came to me where God said this, He told me, 'But I told you to rejoice with those that can overcome. Rejoice with them.'"

Even knowing in advance that the scholarships would do him no good, Hurt would do it all again. Ride the school bus to Richmond, speak on the steps of the Capitol—just to help win the fight in the General Assembly for others to benefit. "I rejoice with them. Most of us are real tight," he told me.

Looking at his present circumstance, Hurt acknowledged, "I'd be lying if I told you it's where I want to be. It's not where I want to be, but I'm glad I'm not where I used to be. Ken, when I came to you [in 2003], I could hardly write my name. I could hardly read the scriptures. It took time . . . but I haven't picked the Bible up yet with a sermon that I didn't get. I tell people, 'I don't have nothing for you, but if God give it to me I'll give it to you.'"

I told him that he had made the *Brown* Scholarship crusade personal for me, had given me a specific person to fight for, and how that kept me going when I felt overwhelmed by the political machinations and fatigue. Apparently, I'd had a similar effect on him.

"I'm telling you this—it was you that caused me to never lose hope. I said many times, 'Man, if Ken can believe in me and go to bat for me like this' . . . That encouraged me to march on."

Hurt continued to be tutored in reading once a week. He never had, and never would, give up. He hoped to finally be able to use a *Brown* Scholarship in 2016 after he retired from VDOT.

"Right today," Hurt said, "I'm not yet where I want to be, but I'm striving. I'm striving. Right today I can tell you some people that went to school, that went back to school [in 1964] and did graduate and today they can't do what I can do. They were just pushed through school because of their age and size."

The complete absence of anger or bitterness in Hurt is profound.

"Everybody didn't overcome. Everybody didn't overcome. They really didn't. A lot of people gave up hope," Hurt said. "But guess what? The biggest thing I like about it, Ken—when I stop and look at it—in the physical and the natural, I should be a hater. I should hate the system for what they done to me. But I don't. I don't. Really, I don't. I do not hate the system."

In the *physical and the natural*—the way human nature most often manifests itself—anger and bitterness would consume Hurt. The telling fact that he is most pleased, above all else, about the lack of hatred in his heart is the fingerprint of Hurt's soul. His distinctive identity.

If only the Founding Fathers had possessed the courage to give Hurt's ancestors a chance. How different it all would have been. The white borders framing the world of Prince Edward County in the 1959 Polaroid photo of me would have meant nothing. John Hurt and I could have been children playing on the green grass under a blue sky together.

"I'm real proud of where I come from," Hurt said of his journey through and out of massive resistance.

"I think my sorrow made me what I am."

In 2016—his last chance—John Hurt applied for and received *Brown* Scholarship funding. New applications would no longer be considered to ensure there is sufficient money in the reparation program for presently enrolled participants to complete their chosen educational journeys. At age sixty-five, John Hurt had finally joined them. At the time of this book's publication, he was still using the scholarship program to continue his own journey.

14

'For All Wounds Known and Unknown'

On an evening so hot it could have baked bread, the block of Farmville's Main Street in front of the Prince Edward County courthouse was closed to vehicular traffic. But it was wide open to people who had come for a communion of healing.

The Light of Reconciliation would soon shine atop the courthouse for the first time and the words of its memorial marker would fill the air. On July 21, 2008, Prince Edward County was formally, publicly, and permanently confronting its past.

On April 13, 2004, the Prince Edward County Board of Supervisors had adopted a resolution that became part of the county's historical record. The words had their moment in the sun but were then filed away with the minutes of that meeting, eventually consigned to the large, bound editions of Board of Supervisors records. That is the usual fate of most resolutions adopted by any governing body.

But this had been no ordinary resolution.

In conjunction with the fiftieth anniversary of *Brown v. Board Education*, the Board of Supervisors adopted a resolution noting that

> between 1954 and 1959, the Commonwealth of Virginia's strategies for avoiding integration included "massive resistance" . . . In 1959, Prince Edward County appropriated zero dollars for public education resulting in the closing of all public schools in the County.

The first of the resolution's four "be it resolved" statements was:

[W]e, the undersigned members of the Board of Supervisors of the County of Prince Edward, Virginia, hereby regret that decisions of the past have adversely shaped the lives of many citizens of our County.

The three other statements recognized the "courage and personal sacrifice made by citizens" of the county, affirmed the Board's "commitment to defend the rights and liberties of our citizens," and recognized the supervisors' commitment "to providing quality public education and equality in education to all children of Prince Edward County."

The vote to adopt the resolution was unanimous.

They were good words, with the potential to become important steps toward the community's ongoing journey of healing and reconciliation. But whatever public impression the resolution made was short-lived. The resolution went out of sight, out of mind. In the spring of 2008, some in the community were calling on the Board of Supervisors to apologize on behalf of Prince Edward County for massive resistance.

THE IDEA FOR A "light of reconciliation" came to me during a walk on the Wilson Trail through the woods at Hampden-Sydney College on May 8, 2008. That week I had gone to Richmond to observe one of the final planning meetings for the Commonwealth of Virginia's Civil Rights Memorial. The memorial on the grounds of the Capitol would be unveiled on July 21 and would depict Barbara Rose Johns, L. Francis Griffin, Oliver Hill, and Spottswood Robinson. As I walked, a thought came to mind. Prince Edward County, their own community, had never honored Barbara Rose Johns and her classmates for the nation-shaping civil rights history they had made.

I took the idea directly to the county. I had known for years, respected, and trusted Prince Edward County's assistant county administrator, Sarah Puckett—who had grown up in Prince Edward. That day, I emailed Puckett: "Before I suggest this editorially or to anyone I wanted to make the pitch directly to you, giving the Supervisors and Prince Edward County first crack at it."

I told her the "redemptive symbolism" of what I was proposing would be priceless: "A Light of Reconciliation in or on the tower atop the courthouse, the lighting to coincide with the unveiling in Richmond at the Capitol in July of the Civil Rights Memorial, which has so many Prince Edward civil rights heroes in it. A beacon to honor those from Prince Edward who gave so much to change this nation, and a light to continue [guiding] this generation and those to come. A memorial and a trail blaze."

Puckett immediately embraced what she described as a "terrific and important idea!" She suggested I take it informally to a member of the Board of Supervisors, Mattie P. Wiley, for her to propose to fellow supervisors. I would be in attendance at the board's May 13, 2008, meeting to explain the concept. Wiley, an African American, had been among those locked out of school in Prince Edward by massive resistance. Her enthusiasm was palpable.

The Board of Supervisors unanimously endorsed the Light of Reconciliation on May 13, and Chairman William G. Fore Jr. appointed a seven-person committee to develop and implement the idea. Fore, a former advertising manager at the *Farmville Herald* who still sold ads part-time, named three Supervisors, Wiley, Howard F. Simpson, and Sally Gilfillan; and citizen members Rita Odom-Moseley, Flossie Hudson, R. R. Moton Museum Executive Director Lacy B. Ward Jr., and myself. We had a lot of work to do in a short time because we wanted to hold the Light of Reconciliation ceremony on the evening of July 21, 2008—fewer than three months away—to complement the state's unveiling that same day of the Virginia Civil Rights Memorial.

The most important decision was choosing the words that would permanently declare the meaning of the light that would perpetually shine in the bell tower atop the county courthouse. A large bronze memorial marker would be installed on the courthouse lawn, below the Light itself. Without those permanent words, the light in the bell tower would have no meaning. It would suffer the same fate of the resolution in the minute books.

I had composed words for the committee's consideration but at that point the Light's true potential had not occurred to me.

Illuminated in the courthouse cupola on July 1, 2008 by the County of Prince Edward in honor of Barbara Johns and the students of R. R. Moton High School for their historic role in ending public school segregation in the United States. When we raise our eyes to see this light, may we also incline our hearts and minds to shine our own light of reconciliation toward all people.

That was my initial draft.

Then it came to me: The county could take advantage of the Light of Reconciliation to emphatically, publicly, and permanently express its sorrow for closing the schools in 1959. I was so aflame with the possibility that I came into my office to email Puckett, canceling what my wife and I had planned for a three-day weekend.

In that May 16, 2008, email with the subject head "6 words for history," I told Puckett,

> I personally believe it is the moment to do this, once and for all, for Prince Edward County forever and ever . . . At some point in the future some Board of Supervisors will have to do this . . . and perhaps at the point of a loaded public gun and petitions, which would rob it of its power . . . This will simply state in direct terms what the Board implied in 2004 . . . Six words to say it all forever. And to give the Light of Reconciliation a depth of meaning it would not otherwise have. I believe we should, and hope and pray we do.

The six words were: "And in sorrow for closing schools."

Puckett agreed. "I love your words and am with you 100 percent," she replied that same day.

The Light of Reconciliation committee agreed, too, also adding the phrase "and all children of the county." On May 20, this statement—I had changed "in sorrow" to "with sorrow"—was presented to the Board of Supervisors:

> The Light of Reconciliation, illuminated in the Courthouse Bell Tower on July 21, 2008 by the Board of Supervisors of Prince Edward County. In honor of Barbara Rose Johns and the students of Robert Russa Moton

High School, and all the children of the county for their historic role in ending public school segregation in the United States, and with sorrow for closing schools. When we raise our eyes to see this light, may we also incline our hearts and minds to shine our own light of reconciliation toward all people.

Supervisor Wiley, our committee chairman, asked the supervisors to approve the wording as presented. The board did so without qualm. "I think it's wonderful," Supervisor Sally Gilfillan, one of the committee members, said prior to the Board's unanimous May 20 vote of approval, as reported in the *Farmville Herald*.

I left that meeting feeling every goal had just been accomplished. Barbara Rose Johns and her classmates would be honored and the words "with sorrow for closing schools" would forever stand front and center in the most prominent place in Prince Edward County—the center of downtown Farmville. The Light of Reconciliation would become one more indelible moral marker.

In a front-page story in the *Farmville Herald*, I provided the full text of the statement and wrote this: "Five words—'with sorrow for closing schools'—expresses in clear, direct and unmistakable language the feelings contained in part of a resolution that the Board of Supervisors adopted on April 13, 2004."

A follow-up story atop the *Farmville Herald*'s front page on June 20 declared in a headline with letters an inch deep: "PE Sups Express School Closing Sorrow." The subhead stated: "Words of Apology Included With Light of Reconciliation."

I wrote that the phrase "with sorrow for closing schools" would be "the County's first direct, explicit expression of sorrow for the 1959 decision to close schools rather than integrate . . ."

The reverse side of the memorial marker would contain the "therefore let it be resolved" climax to a formal Light of Reconciliation Board of Supervisors' resolution. I composed the most emphatic statement I could and won committee approval of every word:

Now, therefore let it be resolved, that we, the undersigned members of the Prince Edward County Board of Supervisors, believe that the closing of public schools in our county from 1959 to 1964 was wrong; and we grieve for the way lives were forever changed, for the pain that was caused, and for how those locked doors shuttered opportunities and barricaded the dreams our children had for their own lifetimes; and for all wounds known and unknown, we do apologize.

That wording was forwarded by the committee to the Board of Supervisors for consideration and action during its regular July 8, 2008, monthly meeting. Meanwhile, from a window in my office each day, I watched county workers add lighting and paint to the bell tower atop the courthouse to accentuate the Light of Reconciliation.

Then, just prior to that July 8 meeting, I was tipped off that a problem had arisen over the word "apologize." One or two board members were questioning, I was told, whether they could apologize for something they did not do. That startled me. "With sorrow for closing schools" had been easily and unanimously embraced by the Board of Supervisors. Furthermore, no Board of Supervisors member or county official had expressed any reservation to my front-page news stories announcing those words of "apology."

I was torn about whether I should attend the July 8 meeting. I knew that with my passion for this subject, and how my emotion rises in its behalf, it was entirely possible I might escalate the discussion into an argument. While writing editorials, I could channel that emotion in a controlled and focused way. Face to face, I was not so certain and was genuinely concerned that everything might crumble at the last minute. We were just thirteen days from the announced Light of Reconciliation event. I decided it would be best if I left matters in God's hands.

The next morning, I learned that the Board of Supervisors had decided to conclude with "we regret those past actions," rather than "we do apologize."

Page 43 of the Prince Edward County Board of Supervisors minutes of the July 8, 2008, meeting shows that our committee chairman, Supervisor Wiley, presented the resolution as drafted and approved by the committee. The minutes record that she told the supervisors,

I would like to offer up an amendment to that resolution based on conversations we've received. We recognize that while we as individuals each
have our own feelings of sorrow for . . . the closing of the schools, and
that we collectively as a governing body may not feel entitled to apologize
for the decision made by previous boards. Therefore, we would like to
recommend adoption by the Board of the amended resolution and I will
make that, make this recommendation in the form of a motion.

The motion carried 7 to 1, with Lacy B. Ward Sr. voting against the
wording change. Ward, one of the board's three African Americans, was
the father of Light of Reconciliation committee member and Robert Russa
Moton Museum Executive Director Lacy B. Ward Jr.

Significantly, the board reaffirmed the Light of Reconciliation's wording
for the Main Street-facing side of the memorial marker that same night—in
fact, it was added, virtually word for word, as a "Be it further resolved" clause
to the board's Light of Reconciliation resolution—keeping the phrase "with
sorrow for closing schools." As it would appear on the memorial marker,
that statement is clearly from Prince Edward County. Anyone reading it
would know the government entity that is the County of Prince Edward
is expressing its "sorrow for closing schools." The wording is stronger—in-
tentionally so—than the slightly passive and detached "with sorrow for the
closing of schools" because it takes full ownership and responsibility for
closing schools. Massive resistance wasn't an act of God or something that
simply happened. Prince Edward County had done it.

The memorial marker's reverse-side wording, on the other hand, would
bear the individual names of the Board of Supervisors. As the board did
in its 2004 resolution, supervisors made certain everyone knew they had
nothing to do with massive resistance. It was an action of the "past."

Though disappointed, I did not believe the board's revision destroyed
the message or meaning of the Light of Reconciliation and its words
that would be forever displayed on the courthouse lawn in the center of
Farmville. An apology, by definition, is an expression of sorrow, regret or
remorse. The Light of Reconciliation directly expresses that on each side
of the memorial marker.

I took great solace that all the other words won the Board of Supervisors' approval:

"We, the undersigned members of the Prince Edward County Board of Supervisors, believe that the closing of public schools in our county from 1959 to 1964 was wrong . . ."

This was a straightforward condemnation of Prince Edward County's massive resistance to *Brown.*

"And we grieve for the way lives were forever changed . . ."

Grief goes beyond even sorrow. The word "grieve" was deliberately chosen for that reason. And that grieving is extended:

"For the pain that was caused . . ."

"For the way those locked doors shuttered opportunities . . .

"And barricaded the dreams our children had for their lifetimes."

The grief expressed by those board members is then, finally, extended to beyond even what the eye can see and the mind imagine:

"And for all wounds known and unknown."

I do not believe the meaning and message of such frank, powerful, and heartfelt words of condemnation and grieving can be destroyed by one word—"regret"—that is, in fact, one of the most common definitions of apology and the word chosen by the Virginia General Assembly for its own massive resistance apology in 2003.

The 2008 Board of Supervisors, which made the Light of Reconciliation a reality—the light and its explicitly declared meaning—was comprised of these six men and two women: Chairman William G. Fore, Vice Chairman Howard F. Simpson, Sally W. Gilfillan, Robert M. Jones, Charles W. McKay, James C. Moore, Lacy B. Ward Sr., and Mattie P. Wiley.

They did a good thing.

ON THE SMALL STAGE erected in front of the Prince Edward County courthouse steps, members of the county's Board of Supervisors sat in chairs as the sun set on July 21, 2008. With them were several invited speakers, including Leslie Francis "Skip" Griffin Jr., Joan Johns Cobbs, and Marcie Wall. Each would share words about what the Light of Reconciliation meant to them.

Farmville's Main Street was brimming with people, black and white together. The vast majority of the four hundred folding chairs provided by the county were filled. Other attendees stood. The response by the community to the dedication of the Light of Reconciliation was overwhelming. And everyone in attendance was provided with a copy of the Light of Reconciliation resolution to take home with them. Those who weren't there could feel as if they had attended through Rob Chapman's front-page coverage in the *Farmville Herald*.

Griffin, whose father, the late Reverend L. Francis Griffin, led the black community during the civil rights era, was in the sixth grade when schools closed in Prince Edward. He traveled from Massachusetts to witness the unveiling of the Virginia Civil Rights Memorial and participate in the Light of Reconciliation ceremony. Standing at the lectern, Griffin first addressed a question raised earlier: Why now?

"We have a saying," Griffin said in his baritone voice, "God may not come when you want him to come but He's always on time. So I say, Why *not* now? Any moment that God's chosen for us to reach out to each other to try to reconcile with one another is the right time. And I think it's incumbent upon all of us to embrace that moment.

"Reconciliation is never easy. It requires everyone to look into his or her heart and to decide," he said, "what kind of world is it that I want to live in? What kind of world is it that I'm willing to work for?"

Speaking, he said, from the lessons he'd learned from his father, whose sermons he'd heard every Sunday at First Baptist Church, Griffin noted the ceremony was taking place framed by that church located on Main Street one block away and Farmville Baptist Church, right beside the courthouse. He didn't have to say what everyone knew—First Baptist is a historically black church and Farmville Baptist is a historically white church.

Griffin offered the crowd two lines from "a prayer that we recite in both these churches. We're all familiar with that prayer and the two lines I refer to are 'On earth as it is in heaven.' The second line is 'forgive us our trespasses as we forgive those who trespass against us.'"

Addressing both sides of the reconciliation divide, Griffin said, "It's easy to point to people who have hurt us. But before we do that I'd ask you to look into your hearts and think about the times when you've hurt somebody.

Maybe not on a political level, but on a personal level. And what would it mean to you to have that person forgive you."

"Forgive us our trespasses as we forgive those who trespass against us," he continued, delving deeper into the Lord's Prayer, "is not just a line that applies to your personal life. That's a line that applies to communities, commonwealths, nations, and the world."

No, reconciliation will not be easy, acknowledged Griffin, who had heard Dr. Martin Luther King Jr. speak at his father's church on March 28, 1962. "Every step will not be firm. Some steps will be tentative. We will stumble and fall. We will be tempted to backtrack," he said.

But the attempt must be made and it requires active, persistent engagement.

Reconciliation, he stressed, is not something that can be accomplished from the sideline. "The real question," Griffin repeated to emphasize the point, "is what are you willing to do? What am I personally willing to do to restore to wholeness? That is the task that is before us."

The task, moreover, before human beings who are created in God's image.

"But the question is—what *is* the image of God? It's not a physical image," said Griffin. "It's the ability to love, to reach out and touch one another, and to connect with that which is basically human in all of us. It is about respect, about the recognition of our common humanity, about our ability to rise to the heavens, but sometimes to fall and not be perfect and to ask for forgiveness. And to be granted forgiveness. It is about accepting that we are all the result of God's unlimited love and His amazing grace."

Reconciliation, he continued, will proceed most effectively "if we talk to one another as 'I and thou' and not 'I and it' or 'I and another.'

"The truly daring," he said, "are not those who dream of conquest, but, rather, those who look to the future, join hands with their brothers and sisters and say, 'We can make this world a better place.'"

MARCIE WALL, GRANDDAUGHTER OF J. Barrye Wall Sr. and the cousin of my publisher, Steven E. Wall, eagerly accepted when I called her with the invitation to speak during the ceremony. Her presence contributed to a powerful point that might nonetheless have gone unnoticed amid the evening's proceedings. She made certain everybody recognized the meaning of the three families who were looking out at them.

"Who would have thought it? A Griffin, a Johns, and a Wall on the same stage at the same time supporting the same cause," said Wall, who, like Griffin and Barbara Rose Johns's sister, Joan, had traveled from out of town, returning to Prince Edward to participate in the Light of Reconciliation ceremony. "Oh my, how times have changed."

What happened in 1959, she continued, "split apart a family. This one. My home, which had operated for many years as a family, maybe a dysfunctional one at times but a family nonetheless. And like many families, this community had disagreements and sometimes even arguments but it was a family and it's becoming a family again . . . Here we are in 2008 . . . building bridges to forge a better future for our children and their children."

A young child when schools closed, Wall remembered accompanying her father to his law office in the courthouse one day and encountering protesters. Her father, the late J. Barrye Wall Jr., was an attorney and older brother of William B. Wall, both of them sons of the late J. Barrye Wall Sr. The young girl didn't understand then what was going on that morning. "I asked my father," she said. "He did not answer."

Her father's silence was not born from ignorance. Like his father and younger brother, he supported defunding the public school system in massive resistance to *Brown*.

"It really stuck with me," Wall said of the scene that day and the silence of her father. "I remember it clearly today as if it had happened yesterday."

The protesters had been seeking an end to massive resistance. J. Barrye Wall Jr.'s wife, Marcie's mother, Jackie, was opposed to the closing of schools and the couple was not silent on the subject with each other.

"The act of closing public schools ripped this community, this family, apart. And it caused great strain in families, too. I remember my parents having vehement discussions on integration and related topics," recalled Wall.

"And now this, this beacon, this light of reconciliation, what a wondrous step, what a way to honor the past and those [Barbara Rose Johns and her classmates] who took a risk," continued Wall, whose side of the Wall family had nothing to do with the daily operations of the *Farmville Herald*. "What a way to point this community, this family, my family, toward the future together. What does this moment mean to me? More than mere words can express. When I read in the *Farmville Herald* of the coming of this light my heart was filled with joy, overfilled with joy . . ."

Describing her late mother, Jackie, as "an ardent supporter of equality and integration," Wall said that her mother's reaction to witnessing the evening's event would have been to shout "Hurrah! Hurrah!"

So, shouted Wall, "Hurrah! Hurrah! Well done, Prince Edward!"

Coming from the granddaughter of the man whose editorials five decades earlier had fired the white community's determination to close schools rather than integrate them, those words resonated up and down Main Street, the sky a deepening blue as the sun slipped behind the one- and two-story shops and businesses lining the small-town main street. It felt almost like a vesper light, however, because what was happening now, after what occurred in 1959, was anything but typical. Evensong, it seemed to me, had been sung by Griffin and Wall.

PRINCE EDWARD COUNTY SCHOOL Board Chairman Russell Dove, the first African American to hold that position in the county, was also asked to speak and told those gathered for the ceremony that, "To me, this light is a symbol that the current Board of Supervisors is officially recognizing that their counterparts in 1959 made a devastating error in judgment when they withheld the operating funds and locked the doors of the public schools."

The location of the Light of Reconciliation was stressed by Dove, as well. "It's important that this symbol will be illuminated from this courthouse . . . It was from this location that the unthinkable decision was solidified in 1959. I am confident this light will generate opportunities for good discussions for some, but for others, it will serve as a reminder of a painful and shameful past. . . ."

Dove did not have to read about that past. He lived it. Like Griffin and Wall, he was a youngster during massive resistance. As he thought about what the light meant to him and what he would say about it, Dove found himself traveling back to his "yesteryears" and he could not escape one thought.

"I thought of what the light could not provide me," he said.

The Light of Reconciliation, he explained, "cannot recover the years of growing up in my Rice home without my eldest brother. Although I had many other siblings . . . the childhood memories and the sibling bond between my eldest brother and I were forever changed. My brother was forced to leave home to continue his education."

And he'd never returned to live in Prince Edward. Likewise, some of Dove's friends and classmates disappeared from his life, as they, too, were sent away to attend schools in communities where public schools were not defunded, shut down, padlocked, and bordered by no-trespassing signs.

But the Light of Reconciliation also brought Dove's mind to thoughts about the present and kindled thoughts about the future.

"In spite of that," he said, regarding the impact of massive resistance on his life, "I stand here with enthusiasm . . . enthused about the possibilities that lie ahead . . . What does the light mean to me? It means that it is possible that this symbolic event can be used as a catalyst to future acts of reconciliation, acts that will truly illuminate Prince Edward."

A NEW DAY IN Prince Edward must be steeped in the knowledge and acknowledgment of the county's past, Board Chairman Fore declared. Quoting Abraham Lincoln's observation that "We cannot escape history," Fore said, "Prince Edward County cannot deny its past. And we cannot, and should not, try. I think we must embrace it and I think we must learn from it. Without that knowledge, we as a community risk repeating what earlier generations have paid so dearly to learn . . . Each day, each of us must find the courage to challenge those who carry divisiveness and prejudice. Collectively, it will take courage from each of us to pass to the next generation a better community, a better school system, a better Prince Edward County, and a better world, better than the ones we inherited."

One by one, members of the Board of Supervisors then read the words that would appear on both sides of the memorial marker.

Yes, my initial reaction to the Board's decision to replace "we do apologize" with "we regret those past decisions" had been disappointment. "Apologize" is more easily recognized as an apology. But as I sat on the stage listening to Wiley and Fore recite the pair of statements that conclude the board's

Light of Reconciliation resolution and unambiguously state its purpose, I asked myself two questions. The answers weren't hard to find.

Does The Light of Reconciliation contain the word "apologize"? No.

Does it express words of apology? Yes.

Some members of the Board of Supervisors clearly felt they could not apologize, by name, for the massive resistance imposed by others. But, with their embrace of the Light of Reconciliation and adoption of its words for permanent public display, they allowed the County of Prince Edward to do so. The words read by Wiley and Fore clearly express that, without the risk of someone reading the memorial marker and, seeing their names, wondering if those board members had been responsible for what they were apologizing for.

As County Administrator Wade C. Bartlett explained to me in the summer of 2017, "the County's stance has not changed as to the reason for the editing of the wording of the resolution. Because the closing of the schools occurred almost fifty years prior to the construction of the Light of Reconciliation there was concern that if the wording was not precise those not involved in that decision could be tainted."

Bartlett had been extremely supportive and helpful in bringing the Light of Reconciliation to fruition. "The Board approved the change," he added, reiterating what he had told Dionne Walker of the Associated Press in 2008, "to avoid assigning blame to those who weren't directly involved in that unfortunate decision."

What I had not taken into consideration while composing the wording for the memorial marker's reverse side was the way any person might react to having their names forever enshrined in bronze following the words "we do apologize" for a terrible thing that they, themselves, had not done. I should have been more sensitive to that and used language that clearly distanced the current board from that dark past.

After reading the words that would face out toward Main Street, Chairman Fore asked the late Barbara Rose Johns's sister, Joan, to step forward. It was her honor to light a candle on stage that would signal county staff to illuminate the Light of Reconciliation.

Applause filled Main Street as the light shone its beacon for the first time and, following the final notes of a benedictory hymn, Cobbs stepped up to the microphone: "This is a moment I am experiencing in my lifetime and it's hard to believe, but I'm very grateful."

Cobbs had traveled from New Jersey and had been present at the unveiling in Richmond of the Virginia Civil Rights Memorial earlier in the day. "And I want to say," she concluded with a shout, looking up toward the heavens, "Barbara, this is for you!"

Even in the darkness, the twinkling joy in her eyes was as obvious as the light now shining under the star-filled night sky, offering an entirely different fallout across Prince Edward County than was triggered in 1959.

"THE EVENT WAS AWESOME AND UNFORGETTABLE!!" Cobbs wrote, using all caps in her email to me on July 23. "Lighting that candle—and causing the light in the bell tower of the courthouse building to come on at that moment—was very emotional for me! Thanks for giving me the privilege to do that! I feel that Barbara's spirit was present there, as well."

Three months later, the Light of Reconciliation would reach as far as Paris. In the French daily newspaper *La Croix*, Gilles Biassette would conclude his November 3, 2008, story on Prince Edward County's painful civil rights history and Barack Obama's campaign to become the first black president in the U.S. by citing "la lumiere de la reconciliation" atop the county's courthouse.

As is true with human darkness, there is no limit to how far our light might travel, once we give it a chance.

ELEVEN MONTHS LATER, THE seven-foot-tall Light of Reconciliation bronze memorial marker was unveiled during an evening ceremony that again closed Farmville's Main Street to traffic so that it might fill with people. It was June 3, 2009, fifty years to the day since the county's Board of Supervisors voted to shut its public schools.

Earlier that day on the floor of Congress, Virginia's Fifth District congressman, Democrat Tom Perriello, addressed the Light of Reconciliation and its meaning.

"As long as inequality and suffering persist in our nation and the world, our work is incomplete. This memorial not only looks back to the dreams deferred by locked schoolhouse doors, but also forward to a better nation, one of ever-expanding opportunity for all," Perriello told Congress, as I reported in my coverage of the event for the *Farmville Herald*. "Martin Luther King Jr. once said, 'Darkness cannot drive out darkness; only light can do that.' Let this light in Prince Edward County, Virginia, be a permanent reminder of our ongoing struggle for a fairer world."

A statement by former governor and now U.S. Senator Mark Warner was also read. "I congratulate the Prince Edward County Board of Supervisors for apologizing for the wrongs of the past," Warner wrote, recognizing the Light of Reconciliation's meaning and message, "and dedicating a memorial that will encourage public discussion and help to heal the wounds of the past."

Prince Edward County School Board Chairman Russell Dove reprised his speaking role from the previous year's dedication and illumination ceremony. He refuted any suggestion, I noted in my front-page story for the *Farmville Herald*, that the Light of Reconciliation is "too little too late . . . As a lifelong citizen of Prince Edward County, I applaud the decision to place this memorial on the courthouse lawn. For me, it's important that we honor the courage, sacrifices and the resilient nature of our citizens, those who not only made Prince Edward a better place but they helped shape our nation's educational system."

I remembered how massive resistance forever changed the human topography of family, love, and friendship in Dove's life. Brothers torn apart, the life they could have shared together a wondered at memory of something that never was, something just beyond reach, like awaking mid-dream and believing, for a moment, that its happy landscape is your world. For me, that made Dove's perspective resonate with truth.

The crowd had gathered beneath menacing clouds. People had come despite severe thunderstorm alerts across the area. But those storms never came. They passed in the distance, unseen and unheard as the double-sided Light of Reconciliation memorial marker was unveiled, as scheduled, before twilight so that all of those assembled could read what was now set permanently in bronze on the courthouse lawn in the center of Farmville.

In the end, after so much had been written and said about it, the Light of Reconciliation would now, and forever, speak for itself.

The gray clouds hastened the feel of approaching darkness. Atop the courthouse where the decision had been made to destroy Prince Edward County's public school system in 1959, the Light of Reconciliation shone with increasing brightness as the gloaming began to fade. Many lingered, waiting in line to read and contemplate the words on both sides of the memorial marker.

Waiting on the bright edge of the gathering darkness.

A darkness that in 2009 was only the night.

Epilogue: Will We Live Happily Ever After?

Driving near Darlington Heights today, I pass the state's historical marker at the birthplace of the Reverend Vernon Johns:

> A blunt-spoken opponent of racial segregation and a champion of civil rights, Johns exhorted his congregations to resist the laws that constricted their lives.

Johns immediately preceded Martin Luther King Jr. as pastor at Dexter Avenue Baptist Church in Montgomery, Alabama. Reverend Johns, who had moved from Darlington Heights to accept the pulpit in Alabama, is buried not far from his historical marker. In addition to being a powerful preacher and a forerunner of the civil rights movement, Johns was the uncle of Barbara Rose Johns. Shortly after the 1951 student strike in Farmville, Barbara was sent to Montgomery to live in the Dexter Avenue Baptist Church parsonage with her Uncle Vernon and Aunt Altona, a music teacher and accomplished pianist. One of her cousins wrote me in 2005, recalling Barbara's arrival for sanctuary in 1951. The aftermath of the strike "caused our families to fear for her safety," she said. Barbara would never again live in Prince Edward County.

"I wept as I read in the *New York Times* about [the *Brown* Scholarships]," seventy-year-old Altona Adelaide Johns-Anderson had also told me in a letter mailed from her home on the West Coast. She remembered the *Farmville Herald* of her youth as such a "vile" newspaper "that my parents ordered the *New York Times* and the *Carolina Israelite* for us to read."

A little further down this road, I turn left at a gravel drive, stop the car, and get out to look for what I might find there. There is no sign that Barbara Rose Johns once lived in a home atop the gentle rise of land in front of me. Nothing to tell anyone that right here she'd been inspired to lead her Robert R. Moton High School classmates into civil rights—and American—history.

Nor is there any charred scar in the land to show that the Johns family home was burned to the ground by arsonists in May 1954 in retaliation for the *Brown v. Board of Education* decision, of which the 1951 lawsuit in Prince Edward County following the student strike was a key part. Instead, there is a five-bedroom brick home built beginning in 1991, thirty-seven years after the Johns home place disappeared in flames.

"Barbara insisted," younger sister Joan tells me. "She pushed it as hard as she could. She insisted that we had to do this." Barbara, in fact, drew up construction plans herself. There are five bedrooms, one for each of the siblings, Joan, Barbara, Ernest, Robert, and Roderick.

Joan says the house "is a legacy" from Barbara for the rest of the family, who still gather here for reunions or when one of them visits the county.

PRINCE EDWARD COUNTY'S JOURNEY away from its troubled racial past is not over. Nor is America's. But to say that a community that once endured five years of massive resistance now faces some of the same challenges as communities that did not shows just how far Prince Edward County has come in the decades since the closing of its schools.

During the wave of arson attacks in the U.S. on African American churches in 1995–96, a Unity Day march was organized by my friend Sarah Terry, then executive director of the Farmville Area Chamber of Commerce. Blacks and whites walked together that Sunday evening to show solidarity for the churches that had been burned and to demonstrate that in Prince Edward County the flames of hate no longer had a willing audience.

Indeed, as the community has confronted its past over the past few decades, it has made more progress toward racial healing and reconciliation than have many other places in America. Pulling back the rug and sweeping the dirt of massive resistance out into the open was essential for healing and reconciliation. Prince Edward County sends the nation a far different message today.

In 1965, Bob Smith wrote *They Closed Their Schools* about Prince Edward's then-fresh scars from massive resistance. But in 1997, he wrote hopefully of the community's journey of reconciliation in "Prince Edward County: Revisited and Revitalized," published in the *Virginia Quarterly Review.*

He followed that in-depth article with a lengthy piece in 2011 about the community's continued progress. Writing under the byline of R. C. Smith, he entitled his story: "Prince Edward County and Racial Redemption"; it was published by the Virginia Social Science Association. Smith had been observing Prince Edward County for nearly half a century, and his concluding thought was this:

> . . . In my mind, Prince Edward has become a minuscule of this nation's long and painful struggle to put away historic racial divisions forever. Surely that means that we Americans are gaining in spirit and, increasingly, in deed, in the long battle to lay the ghosts of slavery where they belong, in the murky past—not to be forgotten but to be stripped of their power to cloud our minds and diminish our better selves.

And Evan Osnos wrote in his article "Kaine Country," published in the October 24, 2016, issue of *The New Yorker,*

> . . . in Prince Edward County it was hard not to sense a lesson for the rest of the country—here was no simple fairy tale about rapid reconciliation, or an end to prejudice and fear, but a real-world example of fashioning a new coherence.

JAMES GHEE WAS LOOKING forward to his freshman year in high school when Prince Edward County defunded public education. He was out of school for two years before the American Friends Service Committee, the social arm of the Quakers, found him sanctuary. At the age of sixteen, his journey for academic refuge took Ghee halfway across America to Iowa.

During a public meeting at the Robert Russa Moton Museum on July 14, 2014, to discuss a proposed affiliation between the museum and Longwood University, Ghee, by then president of the Prince Edward County chapter of the NAACP, raised the issue of trust and made the case for Longwood taking ownership of its past. Prince Edward County had apologized for massive resistance, Ghee pointed out, and so had the Commonwealth of Virginia.

Longwood President W. Taylor Reveley IV responded immediately, as I reported in the *Farmville Herald*. "I will see to it," he told Ghee during the meeting, "that Longwood publicly apologizes on the record for what's happened." Two months later, the institution issued a statement headlined: "Longwood expresses regret over institution's actions during civil rights era."

Longwood's board of visitors adopted a resolution acknowledging and expressing its "profound regret" for the university's public silence during massive resistance and the pain inflicted through the use of eminent domain[*] for campus expansion into the adjacent African American neighborhood. The September 13, 2014, resolution offered Longwood's apology to "those who have been hurt."

The proposed formal affiliation between the Moton Museum and Longwood University was finalized the following year. A "Covenant In Perpetuity" will bring additional financial and administrative resources to the museum through its affiliation with the state-supported university.

The covenant, signed June 30, 2015, declares that the mission of the museum located at 900 Griffin Boulevard—renamed by Farmville's Town Council from Ely Street to honor the Reverend L. Francis Griffin Sr.—"shall remain in perpetuity:

> To share the story of the Moton strike and imprint it more deeply on the national consciousness;
>
> To advance and expand public understanding of the history of the struggle for civil rights, in which the Moton struggle played such a fundamental role; and

---

[*]   A practice Longwood abandoned in the 1990s.

To advance the Museum's broader mission of supporting the cause
of civil rights in education.

The Robert Russa Moton Museum anchors the Civil Rights in Education
Heritage Trail that includes forty-one sites and more than a dozen Virginia
counties. The museum's website declares the National Historic Landmark
to be the "Student Birthplace of America's Civil Rights Revolution." The
covenant with Longwood University means that the site of the 1951 student
strike will never stop telling its story.

Barbara Rose Johns did not live to see the Virginia General Assembly
create the *Brown* Scholarships. She never saw the Light of Reconciliation
nor read its words on the courthouse lawn.

"She would be surprised," her sister Joan says. "She would be pleased."

Johns did, however, live to see the foundation dug for the new home
she insisted her five siblings construct on the spot where their childhood
home once stood.

She had married the Reverend W. H. R. Powell. The couple had four
daughters and a son. After earning a master's degree in library science from
Drexel University, she served as a librarian in the Philadelphia public school
system for twenty-four years.

And then she became ill.

"We knew she was sick. But we didn't know she was that sick," Joan
recalls. Cancer came and quickly ravaged her sister. One day, Joan picked
her up in Philadelphia, and Barbara lay on a body-length pillow Joan had
purchased to make her as comfortable as possible during the long trip to
Prince Edward County. Joan said she sensed it would likely be Barbara's last
chance to see the beginning of the new house.

As she looked at the foundation, Barbara Rose Johns Powell would have
had no trouble seeing the finished house in her mind's-eye. She had always
been a woman of vision.

She died September 25, 1991, at the age of fifty-six. The United States
of America was changed for the better because she had lived.

In the May 20, 1994, issue of the *Farmville Herald*, I was able to write in my editorial celebrating the fortieth anniversary of the *Brown* decision: "The headline in the May 17, 1994, edition of . . . *Newsday* reads like this: 'A Model for the Nation, Virginia county has high-quality integrated schools.' The county—the model for the nation—is Prince Edward County." The New York newspaper, then one of the five largest daily papers in America, had published an in-depth series to commemorate the anniversary. The story's author was reporter Timothy M. Phelps, who had visited each of the five communities whose cases were consolidated in the landmark *Brown v. Board of Education* litigation.

I believe a commission should be established to study the generational impact of the school closings and produce a report that could guide county funding and curriculum development to address specifically any continued effects. I made that editorial appeal in the spring of 2014 and have continued follow-up discussions. I hope for the day that assessment is made and utilized for the benefit of the children of Prince Edward County as the community continues its journey of progress.

The school system's resurrection from massive resistance could not have happened without the twenty-five years that Dr. James M. Anderson Jr. spent as the superintendent of the county's schools from 1972 to 1997. The Prince Edward County School Board conference room was named in his honor during a special ceremony on September 12, 2015, an event that also saw the Prince Edward County High School auditorium named for Barbara Rose Johns and the Prince Edward County Middle School gymnasium named for the Reverend L. Francis Griffin Sr. I had urged School Board members to honor the trio by placing their name on school facilities.

In January 2017, Governor Terry McAuliffe announced that the building housing the Virginia Attorney General's office would be named in Johns's honor. "I cannot think of a better person to inspire the men and women who fight for justice and equality in the office of the Attorney General than Barbara Johns," McAuliffe explained.

Once again, someone else's good deed sparked my mind and the relay of light continued. Though I left the *Farmville Herald* at the end of May

2015, after thirty-six years, I remain deeply committed to the community's continued healing. I contacted Farmville Town Manager Gerald Spates and Vice Mayor A. D. "Chuckie" Reid—Reid had been locked out of school during massive resistance—and suggested the community's state-of-the-art public library be renamed in honor of Johns. The idea was warmly received, and Spates told me he believed the town council also would support the name change. The ball was rolling. I was convinced Spates would discuss the proposal with Vice Mayor Reid and Mayor David E. Whitus.

The Town of Farmville—the county seat of Prince Edward County—owns the library building, which was constructed and is funded jointly by the town and county. Assistant County Administrator Sarah Puckett responded via email that honoring Johns in that fashion would be "brilliant." NAACP branch president Ghee also responded with affirming approval. Ghee was keen to see Johns honored in a significant way and had already been mulling over how best to proceed. His embrace of renaming the library after Johns carried great weight with Vice Mayor Reid.

In February, during the council's next regularly scheduled meeting, Mayor Whitus appointed Reid to chair a Barbara Johns Committee to consider how best to honor her. By then, other community voices were urging town action to celebrate Johns and her role in U.S. civil rights history. As owner of the building, renaming the library would be the town's decision—if that proved to be the committee's choice. It was.

On April 12, the council formally renamed the Farmville-Prince Edward Community Library building in honor of Johns. A press release quoted Reid explaining that "Barbara Johns was not only an important figure in our town, but also in the country, and played an integral part of the Civil Rights Movement. Naming the library after her is a way to honor her legacy in our town." Council members Dan Dwyer and Donald Hunter added supportive comments.

The library, located next to Wilck's Lake and on one of the most heavily-traveled four-lane streets in Farmville, is now called the Barbara Rose Johns Farmville-Prince Edward Community Library. The ceremony and sign unveiling occurred on December 10, 2017, and was attended by many members of the Johns family. I was honored, and humbled, to have been asked by

Barbara's sister Joan to deliver the keynote speech during the ceremony.

That a building teeming with the mind-opening, life-changing power of human expression be named in honor of Johns is particularly appropriate. There is no more integrated or more popular public facility for people of all ages in Prince Edward County, and Johns had dedicated her adult life to being a librarian.

The arc of Prince Edward County's journey, I told those gathered at the library that day, "offers living proof, and living hope—not only to the nation, but also to the world—that our lives, that we ourselves, can become human bridges across the deepest chasms."

The former all-white Prince Edward Academy is now Fuqua School, still private but with its enrollment doors now opened wide. "Diversity strengthens a school community and should be embraced," its website states. Fuqua School has a seat on the Robert Russa Moton Museum's Moton Council, the museum's operations and community engagement board, and is an active supporter. Fuqua School students have joined their counterparts from Prince Edward County High School to commemorate the historic April 23, 1951, student strike by walking down Main Street together from the museum to the county courthouse.

Prince Edward County has reason to look toward the future with optimism. So many good people are fully engaged in working together for the community's benefit, gleaning together in the fields of light.

As of 2017, Prince Edward County had an African American sheriff, an African American clerk of court, and an African American commonwealth's attorney—and the latter two are women. For the first time, half of the Board of Supervisors' eight members were African Americans. Election results, of course, are not necessarily revelatory. But it is worth noting in this case that these countywide victories were not the product of a black-majority electorate choosing black candidates. The population of Prince Edward County is 64 percent white and 32 percent black, according to 2015 Census data. President Barack Obama won the majority of Prince Edward County votes in both 2008 and 2012. There was no anti-Obama backsliding four years later, either. Democrat Hillary Clinton edged out Republican Donald Trump among the county's voters, contributing to her popular vote victory in an election she of course ultimately lost in the electoral college.

The young Barbara Rose Johns had dreamed of a "happily ever after" ending for race relations. That *would* be a fairy tale, many might say, looking across a currently polarized America.

The place where Barbara Rose Johns had those dreams by a stream in the woods on the family farm in 1950 and 1951 is now hidden by a nearly impenetrable thicket. Even the old tobacco barn has been swallowed by more than six decades of nature's persistent rambling. Perhaps the naysayers are right to harbor doubts. They may be realists. Every fresh news cycle seemingly confirms their point of view.

In adulthood, Barbara Rose Johns would have had no illusions about the obstacles standing in our way. Life's struggles, however, seemed to have done no more than reinforce her dream with steel. Despite exile from Prince Edward County in 1951 to protect her life, and the destruction of her family's home three years later—despite everything—she insisted her family return to the county and rebuild.

Why should the thought of all of us living happily ever after as Americans be any more unrealistic than trying to form a more perfect union? The Founding Fathers weren't out of their heads when the preamble to the Constitution was written. Indeed, the pursuit of happiness is one of the self-evident truths and unalienable rights highlighted in the Declaration of Independence. A community pursuing happiness together on a daily basis, as so many people are endeavoring to do in Prince Edward County, can find itself living—however imperfectly—"happily ever after," one day at a time. *Happier* ever after than might have seemed possible.

Joy Cabarrus Speakes joined Barbara Johns and the rest of the student body at Robert R. Moton High School in the 1951 strike. She subsequently become a plaintiff in the 1951 *Davis v. County School Board of Prince Edward County* case that helped topple segregated public education in America. As a member of the Commonwealth of Virginia's *Brown v. Board of Education* Scholarship Awards Committee, Speakes knew that the *Brown* Scholarship program was unable to include descendants of those locked out of school by massive resistance. She decided something else needed to be done.

Speakes is a member of the Moton Museum Council and represented the council on the museum's board of trustees. Chair of the council's development committee, Speakes began the Moton Family Challenge fundraiser to support the museum's programming. "In 2016, in furtherance of our mission," she explained, "I added the Moton Family Challenge Scholarship fund."

The fund, the museum's website explained in May of 2017, seeks to annually award renewable merit-based scholarships of $2,500 each to two college-bound high school seniors "who are direct lineal descendants of those affected by the public school closings" in Prince Edward County.

Among the many generous donors are Barrye, Angus, and Geoffrey Wall, cousins of Steven E. Wall, who was my publisher for so many years.

Though their career paths took them away from Prince Edward County, the three brothers have joined the ranks of those actively engaged in the county's journey of healing. (Their sister Marcie played a key role in the Light of Reconciliation ceremony in 2008 and also served on the Moton Council.) The trio made an initial four-year commitment in the spring of 2017 to provide $40,000 to the Moton Family Challenge Scholarship fund. Thus descendants of J. Barrye Wall Sr., who editorialized relentlessly in the *Farmville Herald* on behalf of massive resistance, are now helping further the education of the descendants of those who suffered the consequences of the locked classrooms.

The three men are the sons of the late J. Barrye Wall Jr. and Jackie Wall. Their mother adamantly opposed the massive resistance that their father vigorously supported. Speaking for his two brothers about their scholarship funding commitment, Barrye Wall wrote, "We note that our mother was committed throughout her life to opening the eyes of young people of any race or religion to the world at large through education."

Speakes had met with Barrye Wall during one of his visits to Farmville. They discussed the scholarship fund, which had debuted in 2016 by awarding individual scholarships of $500. Speakes remembers Wall's concern that $500 per student was not as effective as it might be. Wall and his brothers changed that. Their contribution allowed the scholarship program to significantly increase its per-student funding level.

"I always said there was divine intervention in our journey," Speakes reflected. "Barrye and his brothers reinforced my faith in people doing what is right and showing love regardless of the challenge. We are still going through a healing process but I see the community of Prince Edward County headed in a new direction, working together and showing respect and love for each other."

Speakes called the Wallses' generosity "an inspiration to all" and believes it will garner "more support and open more doors of opportunity to those descendants of families whose sacrifice was great. It will also build and unite the community."

I BELIEVE JESUS TOLD the truth. The kingdom of heaven *is* near. It's as near or as far away as we are to each other. I have felt the kingdom's close proximity with John Hurt, John Stokes, Rita Odom-Moseley, Joan Johns Cobbs, and so many others, black and white, as we pursued a more perfect union in Prince Edward County.

The kingdom of heaven was close by as Odom-Moseley and I watched the snowflakes fall on the January night in 2004 prior to our scheduled testimony before a House of Delegates committee. The kingdom of heaven was next to John Hurt as we sat outside the Farmville-Prince Edward Community Library on the evening of September 9, 2015. It was all around John Stokes and me as he took me to the book of the prophet Jeremiah during our February 18, 2003, phone conversation. When Prince Edward County assistant county administrator Sarah Puckett enthusiastically embraced the idea of the Light of Reconciliation, the kingdom of heaven was close enough for both of us to touch. I think Barbara Johns's sister Joan and I feel the kingdom of heaven each time we greet each other with a hug. I am certain it was there, too, with Barrye Wall and Joy Cabarrus Speakes.

Those weren't isolated glimpses, either.

Barbara Johns's cousin with whom she'd taken shelter in Alabama had spoken of something else in her 2005 letter. She recalled being a young girl in Prince Edward in the 1940s, before her father accepted the Dexter Avenue Baptist Church pulpit, and painted a hauntingly idyllic scene I did not expect. A "few white people," Altona Adelaide Johns-Anderson wrote, "visited us after dark to exchange ideas" with her father, "sip brandy, and hear my mother play Chopin and Brahms."

The kingdom of heaven was surely there with them. The tragedy for Prince Edward County is that there wasn't enough room for it anywhere else in the lead-up to and aftermath of the *Brown* decision. No place for it in the light of day.

An even greater tragedy for America would be if we cannot find more room for it in our hearts today.

Hatred too easily segregates humanity along false, manmade borders. In America, from the very beginning, racial division has been the most diabolical. But our ability to love one another must surely give us the chance to cross that divide. And, if God really is love, why wouldn't we try, believing that we can?

And if God is not love, why wouldn't we try anyway?

THE *BROWN* SCHOLARSHIPS CREATED by the Virginia General Assembly and Prince Edward County's Light of Reconciliation point the United States toward several crucial next steps:

- A full, formal national apology for the cancer of slavery and the malignancy of the Jim Crow segregation that followed;
- A National Light of Reconciliation memorial in the National Mall, modeled on Prince Edward County's example;
- And meaningful reparations.

While both houses of Congress have adopted resolutions that offer an apology for slavery, those separate actions in 2008 and 2009 did not produce a national expression of sorrow and regret. A joint act of Congress, signed by the President of the United States, would achieve that goal.

Though both earlier resolutions were meaningful, the words adopted by the House and Senate briefly spoke but then fell silent without an echo. They will have no impact on posterity. Most Americans who knew of their adoption have already forgotten them. Future generations will have no idea the resolutions exist.

Therefore, not only should the President sign a formal national apology for slavery and Jim Crow, he or she should do so on national television in prime time and then read those words for all to hear—make it an unmistakable, unmissable event of coast-to-coast consequence, the moral equivalent of all eyes turned toward Neil Armstrong's first steps on the surface of the moon.

Let it become a giant leap toward one another.

An apology for the terrorism of slavery and Jim Crow—one that is permanently displayed as part of the National Light of Reconciliation— would minister to a wound that remains deep within our nation's soul. We have addressed many of its racist marks and discriminatory manifestations through the *Brown* and *Griffin* Supreme Court decisions, the civil rights movement, and the Civil Rights, Voting Rights, and Fair Housing acts. But we have yet to honestly stand together and do something directly about the torn place in our national fabric.

Returning to the words of the prophet Jeremiah, that is why no new skin has grown over this wound. No physician has come to heal it and we refuse to even acknowledge that the waiting room has been filled to over-flowing for decades.

This particular Gilead should wait no more.

Let us surround a National Light of Reconciliation and its words of apology with statues of men, women, and children, representing all ethnicities, joined hand in hand. A declaration of our interdependence upon each other. An emphatic affirmation that, yes, we do hold this truth to be self-evident: All people are created equal. Without exception. Every race. All ethnicities.

Let ours be the gathered generations that empower this nation to forever speak with the literal voice of its founding ideals. Emphatically. Publicly. Permanently.

That memorial would become a destination where we gather and share enduring moments of reconciliation with one another, a place of figurative and, I am certain, literal embrace.

A place of new skin.

CONGRESS AND THE PRESIDENT can also emulate Virginia's example. "I am sorry," in other words, "and this is what I intend to do about it." The state legislature followed up its resolution of "profound regret" for massive resis-tance in Prince Edward County, and the state's role in the school closings, by creating the *Brown* Scholarships for those who had been deprived of a formal education.

In April 2006, the Washington-based Faith and Politics Institute brought its "Reconciliation Pilgrimage" to Prince Edward County to understand how the community's ongoing journey of healing might help guide the nation. U.S. Senator George Allen of Virginia and U.S. Representative John Lewis (the civil rights legend) of Georgia hosted the event. I was a participant and publicly challenged the two men to lead both houses of Congress to adopt an apology for slavery and establish—as reported by Kathryn Orth in the *Richmond Times-Dispatch* on April 30, 2006—what I described as a domestic Marshall Plan for blacks.

I editorialized in the *Farmville Herald* the following week calling for the national apology and reparations.

"Some react to an apology by saying, 'Ah, but the devil will be in the details,'" I wrote. "Here's a suggestion: Kick the devil out."

The same advice applies to reparations.

Repair the harm in the ways that are open to us today.

Reparations should include a massive investment targeting our inner cities and rural communities with significant African American populations. The funding would focus on the key areas of education, health care, housing, economic development, and infrastructure. We did so much to help rebuild Europe after World War II through the Marshall Plan. Our own country requires a similar degree of commitment to repair the harm done by slavery and that institution's ongoing aftershocks.

That "domestic Marshall Plan" would, of course, include members of all races who are suffering in those communities—including whites. Not solely African Americans whose descendants had been slaves or were handcuffed by the Jim Crow segregation that followed in slavery's wake. Or who may have pieces of their own lives chained today by lingering, institutionalized racism.

Were a domestic Marshall Plan to be color-blind in those targeted inner cities and rural communities—as it morally must—it would increase public and political support while fostering racial reconciliation. The effort to repair the harm done to African Americans would be seen as the impetus to raise everyone together.

And, crucially, the benefits of any additional and more narrowly focused reparations would not be as positive in their impact on African Americans if the communities in which they reside are not invigorated around them—without a rising tide, no boats get lifted.

THERE WILL BE PUSH-BACK against such a program of reparations, certainly, but only the status quo never pushes back.

This is something we can all do together and without getting defensive about it. No, nobody now living in America has owned a slave, but we still live in the course of the human event that was American slavery. As I wrote in the May 2006 *Farmville Herald* editorial calling for a slavery apology and reparations, "Americans have been born into consequences they didn't deserve from actions they had nothing at all to do with. . . . Where we go from here as a people is up to us. We can ignore our opportunity and leave the wound as it is, or we can minister to the world as we find it."

Years later, it's all still waiting to be done.

And far more than financial investment is necessary to repair the harm done by others.

We cannot underestimate the need to liberally invest our *human* currency in one another. History is replete with "sprees" of inhumanity, such as the one that began with the arrival of the first slave ships at Jamestown, Virginia, in 1619. We must become profligate with our humanity toward each other, absolute spendthrifts in our mutual compassion. Otherwise, any attempt at meaningful and enduring reparation fails.

Ultimately, reconciliation begins or ends with each of us. It must wear our own wrinkles and veins or reconciliation goes nowhere. The final and decisive civil war is always fought within the human heart.

Yours and mine.

A place where the prayers of all God's children can be answered.

The landscape through which all balm must first travel before it can reach any Gilead.

My May 20, 1994, editorial in the *Farmville Herald* that moved the legendary civil rights attorney Oliver Hill to write me the letter that so influenced the rest of my life concluded with these words:

The Promised Land is not a destination. We must carry the Promised Land on our backs wherever we go. Every single day.

We cannot erase or change even one sentence of the past. And the future will be written by others.

But the chapters we add to our American story will also become indelible—pointing the narrative in the direction we have the courage and willpower to take it—because this moment is ours.

Afterword

U.S. Senator Tim Kaine

In the Book of Isaiah, the great Old Testament fount of prophecy, we are told of the Kingdom where "[the] wolf will live with the lamb, the leopard will lie down with the goat, the calf and the lion and the yearling together, and a little child will lead them." That prophecy—prefiguring the birth of Jesus—has echoed down the centuries. The truth of these prophecies did not end two thousand-plus years ago. It found a modern incarnation in the courageous witness of Barbara Johns.

I read of Barbara Johns and Prince Edward County when I was a Midwestern kid attending the University of Missouri in the late 1970s. Richard Kluger's book *Simple Justice* had just been published and that masterwork on the legal history of racial segregation in America exposed me to Johns's 1951 walk-out of Robert R. Moton High School. The compelling story jumped off the page and profoundly influenced my decision to go to law school and then move to Virginia to be a civil rights lawyer.

For seventeen years before I got into statewide politics, I fought against racial discrimination in courts all across Virginia and experienced a place in an often uneasy transition from days of segregation into a more inclusive and just state. That transition, nudged along by so many, including my friend Ken Woodley, has made us live more like a Commonwealth—a community where the wealth we hold is truly shared. And it was a child, more than anyone, who started us down the path.

As mayor of Richmond and governor of Virginia, I offered official apologies for the role of these governmental entities in perpetrating slavery and racial injustice. I worked with my longtime friend Mark Warner on the scholarship program for Prince Edward students deprived of an education by the events Ken Woodley describes so well. When Oliver Hill, the pioneering civil rights lawyer who took on the case of the Prince Edward students, died in 2007 just after his hundredth birthday, the family and I agreed that his body would lie in state in the Governor's Mansion and that I would offer the eulogy at his funeral. How poetically just that this great battler for good—viewed as a pariah by some of my predecessors in the office—was now being officially lionized for his fidelity to the best values of our Commonwealth and country.

And I remember the special day in 2008 when we unveiled the Civil Rights monument on Capitol Square featuring Barbara Johns and her fellow students. The monument was the first on these statue-filled grounds to feature a woman, the first to feature an African American, the first to feature a child, the first to feature a civil rights pioneer. And while the other statues on the grounds have men standing atop pedestals of various sizes, the Civil Rights monument has human figures displayed at ground level around a pedestal where a passerby can stand eye to eye with these very real, very ordinary, very extraordinary people. It warmed my heart as governor to look out my office window and see school groups—children are the most common visitors to the Capitol—taking pictures with their arms draped around the statue of Barbara and her classmates and coming to grips with the notion they could be leaders as well.

I travel to Farmville often—in my role as an elected official but also as a Richmonder who enjoys the town, a nearby bicycling trail, and the wonderful Moton Museum. And I had cause to stand on a stage at the local Longwood University in October 2016 as a candidate for vice president of the United States, running with a history-making strong woman. As I made my opening comments, I couldn't help but talk about Barbara Johns because I wanted everyone watching to know her story.

The story would not be as known as it should be but for Ken Woodley. As the crusading editor of the *Farmville Herald*, he kept the story of her work, and the entire journey from pain to reconciliation in his community, very much alive. In his articles, in his advocacy at the local, state, and national levels, in this book, he has been an untiring witness, or in the words of Isaiah "an ensign of the people," heralding the deeper meaning of the Prince Edward story.

This book shows the extent of this labor, the twists and turns, the compromises and momentary disappointments and the slowly growing wisdom of a community—indeed an entire nation—turning from past to future. But the work is never done. And we so need examples to help us persevere in that work. I thank Ken Woodley for giving us such an example.

Bibliography

Atkinson, Frank B. *The Dynamic Dominion: Realignment and the Rise of Virginia's Republican Party Since 1945*. Fairfax: George Mason University Press, 1992.

Becker, Jo. "Bias Victims Get Empathy, But No Funds: Va. Aspires to Offset Massive Resistance." *Washington Post*, February 26, 2004.

Bonastia, Christopher. *Southern Stalemate: Five Years without Public Education in Prince Edward County, Virginia*. Chicago and London: The University of Chicago Press, 2012.

Branch, Taylor. *Parting the Waters: America in the King Years 1954–63*. New York: Simon and Schuster, 1988.

Branch, Taylor. *Pillar of Fire: America in the King Years 1963–65*. New York: Simon & Schuster, 1998.

Brown v. Board of Education Scholarship Program 2013–14 Application Packet. The Virginia Division of Legislative Services.

Couch, Cullen. "Log Cabin Lawyer." *UVA Lawyer* vol. 28, no. 1 (Spring 2004): pp. 22–26.

Farmville Herald. Editorials, op-eds, news stories: 1954–2015.

Green, Kristen. *Something Must be Done about Prince Edward County: A Family, a Virginia Town, a Civil Rights Battle*. New York: Harper, 2015.

Griffin v. County School Board of Prince Edward County. U.S. Supreme Court opinion, May 25, 1964. Complete text: Wikisource.

Griffin, Rev. L. Francis. Letter to William Vanden Heuvel. November 25, 1964. Archives of the American Friends Service Committee, Philadelphia.

Hill, Oliver W. Sr., edited by Jonathan K. Stubbs. *Big Bang: Brown v. Board of Education and Beyond, The Autobiography of Oliver W. Hill, Sr.* Winter Park: FOUR-G Publishers, Inc., 2000.

Holcomb, Dorothy L. *Educated in Spite of … : A Promise Kept*. Farmville: MAKKA Productions, 2012.

Holton, Linwood. *Opportunity Time: A Memoir by Governor Linwood Holton.* Charlottesville: Copyright by the Rector and Visitors of the University of Virginia, published by the University of Virginia Press, 2008.

Johns, Barbara Rose. Twenty-one handwritten pages of autobiographical recollections, discovered by family in 2000. Copy provided to author by Johns's sister, Joan Johns Cobbs.

Kanefield, Teri. *The Girl from the Tar Paper School: Barbara Rose Johns and the Advent of the Civil Rights Movement.* New York: Abrams Books For Young Readers, 2014.

Kennedy, Robert F. Speech at Kentucky's Centennial of the Emancipation Proclamation, Freedom Hall, Louisville, March 18, 1963. U.S. Department of Justice website.

Leiva, David E. "Warner, former governors urge scholarships for students denied schooling." *Associated Press*, February 13, 2004.

Neff, David Pembroke. "The Defenders of State Sovereignty and Individual Liberties." *Encyclopedia Virginia*. Virginia Foundation for the Humanities, 23 October 2013.

Moseley, Rita Odom. *No School: A Place with No School.* Wayne Drumheller, 2017.

Orth, Kathryn. "Allen weighs slavery apology by Congress." *Richmond Times-Dispatch*, June 30, 2006.

Osnos, Evan. "Kaine Country: Tim Kaine's Strategy for Winning." *The New Yorker*, October 24, 2016.

Payne, Will. *Mark Warner the Dealmaker.* Charleston: The History Press, 2015.

Peeples, Edward H., with Nancy Maclean. *Scalawag: A White Southerner's Journey through Segregation to Human Rights.* Charlottesville: University of Virginia Press, 2014.

Phelps, Timothy M. "A Model for the Nation: Virginia county has high-quality, integrated schools." *Newsday*, May 17, 1994.

Schapiro, Jeff. "Governors regret past 'egregious' Va. policy." *Richmond Times-Dispatch*, February 14, 2004.

Schapiro, Jeff. "Warner asks for education funding: He urges $2 million in scholarships for those denied schooling." *Richmond Times-Dispatch*, February 26, 2004.

Smith, Bob. *They Closed Their Schools: Prince Edward County, Virginia, 1951–1964.* Chapel Hill: The University of North Carolina Press, 1965. Republished in Farmville by the Martha E. Forrester Council of Women, 1996.

Smith, R. C. "Prince Edward County: Revisited and Revitalized." *The Virginia Quarterly Review* vol. 73, no. 1. (Winter, 1997): pp. 1–27.

Smith, R. C. "Prince Edward County and Racial Redemption." *The Virginia Social Science Journal* vol. 46 (Spring, 2011): pp. 57–81.

Southern Poverty Law Center. "Civil Rights Martyrs." Website: splcenter.org.

Stallsmith, Pamela. "Kilgore: Fund *Brown* Scholarships." *Richmond-Times Dispatch*, June 4, 2004.

Steck, John C. "The Prince Edward County Virginia Story." *The Farmville Herald*, 1961.

Stokes, John A., with Lois Wolfe, Ph. D. and Herman J. Viola, Ph. D. *Students on Strike: Jim Crow, Civil Rights, Brown, and Me.* Washington, D.C.: National Geographic Society, 2008.

Titus, Jill Ogline. *Brown's Battleground: Students, Segregationists, & the Struggle for Justice in Prince Edward County, Virginia.* Chapel Hill: The University of North Carolina Press, 2011.

Walker, Dionne. "Prince Edward officials express regret for Massive Resistance." *Associated Press*, July 9, 2008.

Walker, Wyatt T. "Fifty-three Hours with Martin Luther King Jr." Southern Christian Leadership Conference archives/records 1954–1970, housed in King Library and Archives, Martin Luther King, Jr. Center for Nonviolent Social Change, Inc., Atlanta, 1962.

Washington Post. "Repaying Segregation's Debt." Editorial, August 5, 2005.

Wilder, L. Douglas. "Why Not State Funds for *Brown* Scholarships?" *Richmond Times-Dispatch*, March 7, 2004.

Yancey, D. "L. Douglas Wilder (1931–)," *Encyclopedia Virginia*. Virginia Foundation for the Humanities, November 11, 2013.

Yancey, D. "Charles S. 'Chuck' Robb." *Encyclopedia Virginia*. Virginia Foundation for the Humanities, January 5, 2014.

Index